ENTINA ARMENIA ARUBA AUSTRALIA AUSTRIA AZERBAIJAN BAHAMAS BAHRAIN

UTAN BOLIVIA BONAIRE BOTSWANA BRAZIL BRITISH VIR... BULGARIA

MAN ISLANDS CENTRAL AFRICAN REPUBLIC CHAD CHANNEL ISLANDS CHILE CHINA

UBLIC DEMOCRATIC REPUBLIC OF CONGO DENMARK DJIBOUTI DOMINICA DOMINICAN

STONIA ETHIOPIA FAROE ISLANDS FIJI FINLAND FRANCE FRENCH GUIANA FRENCH

LAND GRENADA GUADELOUPE GUAM GUATEMALA GUINEA GUINEA-BISSAU GUYANA

ELAND REPUBLIC OF IRELAND ISRAEL ITALY IVORY COAST JAMAICA JAPAN JORDAN

SOTHO LIECHTENSTEIN LITHUANIA LUXEMBOURG MACAU MACEDONIA MADAGASCAR

UE MAURITANIA MAURITIUS MEXICO MICRONESIA MOLDOVA MONACO MONGOLIA

ETHERLANDS ANTILLES NEW CALEDONIA NEW ZEALAND NICARAGUA NIGER NIGERIA

PHILIPPINES POLAND PORTUGAL PUERTO RICO QATAR REUNION ISLANDS ROMANIA

TS & NEVIS ST. LUCIA ST. MARTIN ST. THOMAS ST. VINCENT SAIPAN SAN MARINO

AK REPUBLIC SLOVENIA REPUBLIC OF SOUTH AFRICA SPAIN SRI LANKA SURINAME

DAD & TOBAGO TUNISIA TURKEY TURKMENISTAN TURKS & CAICOS ISLANDS UGANDA

ICAN CITY VENEZUELA VIETNAM WALES WALLIS & FUTUNA YEMEN ZAMBIA ZIMBABWE

HOW TIME FLIES

THIS BOOK IS DEDICATED

TO THE MEN AND WOMEN OF FEDEX,

WHOSE TALENT AND UNWAVERING COMMITMENT TO

SERVICE WILL SURELY MAKE FAST WORK OF

THE NEXT 25 YEARS, TOO.

Toluca, Mexico

FRED SMITH IS THE ONLY MAN I HAVE EVER KNOWN who has created an entire industry.

I remember in the early 1970s when I was a new and young United States Senator from Tennessee and Fred Smith paid a courtesy call. He was fresh out of the United States Marine Corps. I listened patiently as he explained how he was going to start a company that would deliver small packages using Falcon jets to make overnight deliveries.

As he finished his presentation I thought, "This young man is gonna go broke" and I really ought to tell him. But instead he thrived and prospered, and FedEx grew into the largest and most important integrated express transportation network in the world.

Fred Smith and FedEx are a virtual case study in how entrepreneurial America should work. They went from a well-thought-out premise to an established, well-respected company, an integral part of our nation's, and the world's, economy.

With the advent of guaranteed rapid delivery of documents, packages and freight and the concomitant facility for continuous tracking, "just-in-time" inventory systems for industry in the United States and abroad became possible.

The huge success of FedEx is dependent on many things, but I think none is more important than the esprit and attitude expressed by officers and employees, who from the newest courier to the most senior captain still call their company's founder and chairman — Fred.

HOWARD H. BAKER JR.

How Time Flies: FedEx Delivers the 21st Century
ISBN 0-9662543-1-7
Library of Congress Catalog Card Number: 98-70144

First Printing, February 1998
Printed in Hong Kong

Courier Frandise Sdasdny
Czech Republic

Courier Ilker Amac
Istanbul, Turkey

OF PEOPLE AND PASSION

IT'S NEARLY 10:50 P.M. Almost curtain time. The first lights — a series of fuzzy orbs — appear in the distance against the starry Memphis, Tennessee, sky. Down on the ground, the glowing complex of buildings that is the FedEx SuperHub gears for action, like an orchestra warming up. Crews gather on the tarmac. Tug transports rev. Handheld radios crackle with instructions.

In the air, the first lights grow larger and more distinct, followed closely by another set, and behind them still another and another. The sky glows with a string of lights like some floating celestial garland as air freighters from points around the globe bear down like carrier pigeons on a 294-acre patch of Southern soil, center stage in a nocturnal pageant. Engines whine down as the first plane lands, and the 8,000 employees on duty know what that means: It's show time.

At a pace of 85 per hour, planes touch down from all over the world. McDonnell Douglas MD-11s and DC-10s, Airbus freighters, Boeing 727s — 143 aircraft in Memphis alone. Cargo doors swing open and crews with hydraulic elevators and portable conveyor belts attach themselves alongside, extracting Lexan-and-aluminum containers that average 4,000 pounds apiece. Each jet is emptied in as few as 17 minutes. Small tugs with containers in tow zigzag across the tarmac in what looks like a serpentine dance, carefully avoiding other tugs driving with equal speed and purpose toward the Memphis sorting facilities, where as many as 1 million shipments — 30 percent of the total volume in the FedEx system — pass through every night. Boxes that hold computers and contracts and jet engines and birthday presents. Boxes of airbags, cellular phones, contact lenses, live lobsters, plastic joints for hip replacements and parts for military helicopters. Boxes whose contents keep satellites running, assembly lines running, courts running, companies running. The country running. The world running.

Beat the clock: A plane is offloaded at the Memphis SuperHub.

10

Meanwhile, similar activity unfolds at another vast complex half-a-world away. Fired by electricity and anticipation, the FedEx hub at Subic Bay, the Philippines, burns on the edge of the ocean. Out on the tarmac and inside by the conveyors, the hub's 550-plus employees wait for their cue. At 11:46 p.m., right on schedule, it comes. The first inbound aircraft of the night, FedEx flight FX-80 from Kuala Lumpur, swoops down out of the Pacific night.

The Airbus A310s, DC-10s and MD-11s arrive in a rush of sound and movement. They come to Subic Bay from the brightest lights of the Asian economy. Inside their metallic bellies are the guts and brains of the world's high-tech industries, the semiconductors and CPUs and memory chips. Pulled from the planes at one of 12 widebody gates, the cargo begins its journey, and 184 minutes later the first of it will be launched back into the night.

Inside the Paris hub at Roissy Charles de Gaulle Airport, 12,000 boxes are sorted each hour before being dispersed to the trucks and planes waiting outside.

For these highly time-sensitive shipments, a FedEx hub represents merely a brief stop on the way from Santiago to San Francisco, from Boston to Brussels, from Penang to Peoria. In primary sorting stations they begin their march through a labyrinth of chutes, slides, laser scanners and conveyor belts to be sorted and then reloaded onto aircraft bound for their destinations.

Handlers lift boxes from containers. Label facers turn packages upright. Scanners scan. Computer-controlled plastic arms divert boxes off conveyor belts and send them sliding to the next conveyor belt. At Subic Bay, in a climate-controlled warehouse, employees wear white gloves when packaging semiconductors for delivery to America.

Subic Bay hub, the Philippines

"We all pitch in. That's what makes FedEx a step above the rest. Everyone is willing to go above and beyond their basic responsibilities to get the job done."

CAROLYN LAGER, SENIOR CUSTOMER SERVICE AGENT

Ramp Control Administrator Alfred C. Coleman III gets ready for the night's show at the Memphis Control Tower. Sorting at the SuperHub must be done by 2:07 a.m., a time determined by when the plane bound for Maine, the easternmost route in the FedEx U.S. system, must depart to make its morning deliveries.

Each employee on the tarmac, on the loading dock and at the conveyor belts knows his or her part … knows that each step adds up every morning to something extraordinary.

The task of orchestrating this finely tuned machine falls to the Global Operations Center (GOC), located in a subterranean building near the SuperHub known as the Bunker. This is mission control at Federal Express Corporation ("FedEx"). Here, specialists manage one of the largest civilian networks of satellites and computers, 40,000 vehicles, and the world's largest fleet of all-cargo aircraft (more than 600).

The GOC has thought of every problem that could possibly befall FedEx's single-minded dedication to fast, on-time service and has developed contingencies for each one. Sixteen so-called sweep flights — planes only partially loaded — are on hand every night to stop off in cities that have extra freight to be picked up. Each night a partly empty plane, or "flying spare," leaves Portland, Oregon, heading for Memphis so the GOC can divert it to any city between the West Coast and the Mississippi River that has an overflow or where a mechanical failure threatens service.

The data generated by the FedEx information network — each package is scanned and information on it recorded up to 11 times en route — allow the GOC constantly to adjust and fine-tune the ground and air operations. Extra volume during a computer convention in Las Vegas, for example, prompts FedEx to add more planes into that city. Around Mother's Day and Valentine's Day, additional aircraft fly out of Miami and Southern California to carry cut flowers to shops across the United States. Planners work all year to analyze how to improve service — where to add planes, where to add crews, where to save time and how to increase performance during the Christmas season, a crunch time that is more succinctly and less sentimentally known as "peak."

The high-speed letter sort at the Memphis SuperHub

At the same time the GOC directs this performance, it oversees the loading of some 220 huge 40- and 53-foot-long trucks in Memphis. It also coordinates the sort-and-route logistics of 2 million other shipments at sorting facilities that include two regional hubs (in Indianapolis, Indiana, and in Dallas-Ft. Worth), three international hubs (in Paris, Frankfurt and at Subic Bay) and an international gateway in Anchorage, Alaska. Volume at the Paris hub is growing so quickly — 55 percent each year — that FedEx will have a new 90-acre facility there in 1999.

Back out on the Memphis tarmac, the FedEx Control Tower readies for the outbound ballet. Engines wind up. Hydraulic loaders pull away. Cargo doors lock shut. Marshalers slice the night air with lighted orange wands, and the planes inch backward. At 2:18 a.m. — right on schedule — the first plane screams down the runway. For the finale, nine jets depart every six minutes, the sky filling now with blinking red beacons as the aircraft disperse once again into the night sky. At 4:30 a.m., the last scheduled departure leaves, and Memphis sighs. The drama ends. At least until 9 a.m., when planes carrying shipments with two-business-day and three-business-day delivery commitments begin arriving. The matinee.

YVETTE WRIGHT WILL GO TO GREAT LENGTHS —

literally — to make a delivery on time. So when her FedEx van broke down at 9 a.m. in downtown Columbia, South Carolina, after her first delivery, she did what she had to do. She notified dispatch, then started running. She loaded as many shipments as possible onto her hand truck and carried them on foot to their destinations. She returned to the van, reloaded and repeated the process throughout the five-block route. By 10:27 — within minutes of the 10:30 a.m. scheduled delivery commitment — she had dropped off 122 packages at 27 stops. • "I was happy because I got them all off on time," says Wright, a former high school basketball player. Heading back to the van, she waved triumphantly to the mechanic who had gotten it started again. And off she went to her afternoon deliveries. "I didn't think anything of it," Wright says. "I always think about service." • YVETTE WRIGHT, WITH FEDEX SINCE 1995

The 1994 Great Place to Work study, which evaluated 100 companies in such areas as respect, fairness, pride and camaraderie, scored FedEx highest for its commitment to opportunity: Every FedEx employee, the study confirmed, has the chance to take on new challenges and earn special recognition.

16

Ahead of the dawn, this road show touches down all over the United States and across the globe. In city after city, before alarm clocks ring or morning disk jockeys prattle or coffeemakers burble, crews unload FedEx planes. In Omaha, Nebraska, ramp agents swarm to the plane to help handlers roll containers out of the upper deck. On a busy morning at Narita Airport in Tokyo, a ramp manager helps unload boxes onto a conveyor belt. Throughout the system, everyone's goal is the same: 100 percent customer satisfaction.

At each station, vans stand backed up to conveyor belts as couriers stack boxes inside and plan their routes. Then they're off, each package in their care representing the collective efforts of thousands of people the night before. It is not a responsibility they take lightly. A courier in Louisiana wades through flooded streets to get payroll to a customer. In rural Texas a courier has made a point of recognizing his customers' cars so he can flag them down for a delivery. In Ho Chi Minh City, a courier jumps off his moped when he can't get through a crowded Vietnamese market and delivers his packages on foot.

MOVING MOUNTAINS Every day the people of FedEx are reminded why they work at FedEx: the ability to make a difference in people's lives.

"Every package has a story behind it," says Nancy Lacy, a customer service agent in Austin, Texas. "It might be someone's payment on the mortgage or something life-saving." A 15-year veteran, Lacy has seen the big and the small ways FedEx affects lives. While working in West Texas, Lacy witnessed the life-saving power of the company at its most dramatic. FedEx delivered the drill that allowed workers to free Baby Jessica from a well in Midland in 1987. "We were a small market, and we usually just had Cessna planes flying in. But that day a big FedEx jet came in.

Miho Babay
Kyoto, Japan

FedEx's own FXTV is one of the largest private television networks in the world, producing up to 500 programs each year.

All the FedEx employees were at the airport to watch it land. We were so proud."

Such pride runs deep at every level of the company — from senior managers who volunteer to load boxes at the hub during end-of-year peak to the longtime ramp worker who says she is still so excited about her job that she's sure she bleeds purple and orange. This affection stems partly from the fact that FedEx treats its employees with enormous respect, and partly from the knowledge that they don't just work for a company but for a cultural phenomenon. Each day they help realize an idea that has revolutionized the way people live and do business.

The speed and reliability of FedEx have allowed the capabilities of medicine and science to expand and improve — like shipping blood samples overnight for analysis, or radiopharmaceuticals whose shelf lives are measured in hours. Now people can live and work outside major metropolitan areas because they have FedEx, with its exceptional reach and reliability, as their lifeline to the business world. Products, too, can travel in express mode directly from manufacturer to consumer without the need for middlemen and massive storage facilities.

The world is a different place today because more than 140,000 people give their energy, their commitment and their passion to do what seems almost impossible. They make magic more than 3 million times a day, moving the packages that move the economy while the world sleeps. Then they turn around and do it all again the next day.

MICHIGAN

IT WAS 16°F ON JANUARY 28, 1997, when courier John Mozug saw a woman lurch her car onto the curb to flag down his FedEx van near Detroit, Michigan. Mozug thought she must be expecting an urgent delivery. Instead, she pointed desperately to a nearby duck pond. A white Buick Riviera was sinking fast. "I took off my FedEx coat, laid my SuperTracker scanner in the snow and waded in," says Mozug. • He swam 20 feet in the icy water until he reached the car. The woman inside appeared to be in shock, and the door would not budge. Mozug swam back to the shore, numb with cold and fear. He prayed for a miracle. Next thing he knew, the woman had freed herself and was on top of the car. "I can't swim," she said. • "I dove in," says Mozug, who is also a volunteer pastor for the Assembly of God. "I knew I could help." By now the woman had fallen back into the water, and she dipped under twice as he tried to grab her. Finally, Mozug pulled her to the pond's steep bank, where bystanders were waiting with blankets. Mozug returned to his van. "I called dispatch to have someone bring me dry clothes so I could finish my route," he says. His manager sent a substitute instead. • JOHN MOZUG, WITH FEDEX SINCE 1984

WITH SUCCESS COMES RESPONSIBILITY

BY GEORGE BUSH

 Like many people, I really don't remember "life before FedEx." The advent of overnight delivery service revolutionized not only the business world but also how we lived our lives. Suddenly, forgotten birthdays, urgent legal documents, last-minute invitations — they all ceased to be crises. Once again, our world became a little smaller, a little friendlier, a little easier.

FedEx exemplifies the kind of can-do American spirit that the rest of the world so often envies. Like so many success stories, the company began with a small group of people who had a great idea and then had the determination, creativity and resourcefulness to put their idea into action. Because of the company's dedication to service and quality, FedEx was given the prestigious Malcolm Baldrige National Quality Award, established by my esteemed friend to recognize outstanding American companies.

But as much as I admire FedEx's business success, it is really for another reason that I very much wanted to be a part of your 25th anniversary. That is because your company's heart and soul are as big as its rate of growth.

As some of you know, I made volunteerism one of the focal points of my presidency. That's when I first began talking about "Points of Light" and the simple fact that any definition of a successful life must include service to others.

Although every American, as an individual, shares in the responsibility for community service, corporate America certainly should expect to carry the largest load. I'm reminded of what Teddy Roosevelt — one of my favorite presidents — said about America's relationship to the rest of the world: "Much has been given to us and much is rightly expected of us. We have duties to others, and duties to ourselves, and we can shirk neither."

In many ways, the same holds true with corporate America's relationship to their hometown communities. With success comes responsibility, and FedEx is an outstanding example of a company that literally has taken that challenge to heart.

In 1996, in my hometown of Houston, I was honored to present FedEx with the Points of Light Foundation's Award for Excellence in Community Service. It was an honor well deserved. Not only do you provide an invaluable service to your hometown communities, but you also provide a great example to all Americans of what being a Point of Light truly means.

That is why I am very happy to extend my congratulations to Fred Smith and all the people at FedEx on the very happy occasion of your 25th anniversary. I hope the next 25 years are filled with much success, and heart.

GEORGE BUSH SERVED AS THE 41ST PRESIDENT OF THE UNITED STATES.

19

THE WEDDING DRESS was upstairs waiting for her. Her family had begun to gather at her parents' home in upstate New York. The caterer was preparing the reception at a nearby country club. Joyce Mathis-Feigeles should have been thinking about only one thing — her marriage, in four hours, to her boyfriend of four years. But instead she was on the phone, tracking a critical shipment for a pharmaceutical executive traveling in Paris. She wanted to know, had it cleared customs? When she learned all was well, she called the company's shipping manager to let him know.

The shipping manager was stunned that Mathis-Feigeles, an account executive, had taken time on her wedding day to worry about his package. But the company was new to FedEx. "I just wanted to do what was right," says Mathis-Feigeles, who checked on a few more of her customer's shipments while on her honeymoon in Bermuda.

For Mathis-Feigeles, such follow-through was barely worth another thought. But that's because she's at FedEx, where this kind of spirit is as integral as chips are to a computer. Yet five years later the shipping manager still marvels about the wedding-day wonder. The company, meanwhile, has become an $8 million international account with FedEx.

That's the way it has always worked at FedEx. Creating win-win-win situations. A win for employees, a win for customers, a win for the company. All are intricately united and interdependent in one of the founding principles of FedEx: People-Service-Profit. Since the beginning, founder Fred Smith has emphasized that employees need to be treated with respect and dignity. He knows that especially in a service company — where you're only as good as the people who perform the service — you can't have

Courier Ivana de Oliveira
Rio de Janeiro, Brazil

Courier Eric Roussel
Paris, France

"FedEx people do the most they can for the customer, and they make the same effort for each other, like changing their schedule to help another coworker. This type of thing comes naturally to FedEx employees."

ALICE SOLIWODA, SENIOR SERVICE AGENT/SAL

satisfied customers if you don't have satisfied employees. The idea is nothing less than corporate karma. If the company does the right thing for its employees, the employees do the right thing for the customers in the form of better service, and customers stay loyal to FedEx, which increases profits and allows the company to do more for the employees.

"I firmly believe that employee dedication mirrors the extent to which an organization demonstrates its commitment to its people," says Smith, who lives his commitment by devoting 25 percent of his time to personnel matters. One of his main goals is to ensure that management does all it can to empower employees. "When people know what is expected of them, understand that outstanding performance is rewarded and believe they can make a difference because they will be listened to and are allowed to put their ideas to work, they will make a difference," he says.

To make sure employees know what is expected of them, FedEx offers extensive training for each and every position. At any given time, 3 to 5 percent of the FedEx workforce is in training. The company devotes approximately $155 million a year to training, making FedEx one of America's biggest corporate investors in learning activities.

The FedEx philosophy is that an employee can do an outstanding job if he or she is given thorough information on what the job requires and how to perform it. For instance, none of the 4,500 representatives at the 49 FedEx Call Centers worldwide answers one phone call before completing six weeks of training. Because they are the voice of FedEx in so many respects, they strive for omniscience: how to help customers fill out paperwork, check a transit time and much more.

At FedEx, management doesn't just talk, it listens. The computer terminals in FedEx vans owe some of their best enhancements to courier input. Now when the system directs couriers to

FedEx employees, like FedEx shipments, move all around the world, thanks to the company's unique "jumpseating" policy: As long as space is available, employees can reserve a seat on a U.S. or international flight at no cost. Every month, about 14,000 employees jumpseat.

23

SARASOTA

MINNEAPOLIS

When FedEx redesigned its uniforms in 1994, employees from around the world weighed in on the new designs. They completed opinion surveys (distributed in eight languages), critiqued initial sketches and attended 30 focus groups in 15 cities. The fashionable new designs express the international flavor of FedEx. Purple, rather than orange, has become the predominant color, being more flattering to a diverse range of skin colors. To ensure that couriers from Norway to Nicaragua can work in comfort, there is now a better variety of warm- and cold-weather apparel. Best of all, safety is enhanced with the addition of more reflective material.

their next pickup, the calls appear onscreen in the order that shipments are ready. And pickup requests blink if a customer is paying by check, to help the courier remember to collect it.

These are just the type of ideas often featured on FXTV, the company's satellite-television network. It is one of the world's largest private TV networks, broadcasting a five-minute update weekdays to 1,200 FedEx sites worldwide. FXTV is one of the more innovative ways FedEx keeps far-flung employees informed about corporate goals and initiatives. It also lets employees talk back. Several times a year, Fred Smith hosts live broadcasts and opens up the phone lines to employees' unscreened questions and comments. Senior management does this even more often.

WEIGHING IN Management's best listening device may be the Survey-Feedback-Action program, an annual temperature-taking for FedEx. Every employee anonymously scores the company on leadership, pay, job conditions and general satisfaction. Results are tabulated, and within a few days managers get report cards. Then they must sit down with their people to explore concerns and decide on a plan to address them. FedEx takes the survey so seriously that it has built in a certain "ouch" factor, linking management bonuses to scores on the leadership section.

Among the most popular outgrowths of the survey is the Bravo Zulu, named after the U.S. Navy term for "well done." The program arose when managers said they wanted to reward outstanding effort without going through a formal process. On the spot, they can hand out theater tickets, dinner certificates and cash (up to $100). In fiscal 1997, 111,736 Bravo Zulus were awarded, totaling $7.5 million. The Five Star Award goes to 300 or so employees each year who have made a major contribution to FedEx, with awards running in the thousands of dollars.

FedEx aggressively promotes from within, believing that people who have performed the jobs

BRAVO ZULU
FedEx
Federal Express
World On Time
NO CASH
FedEx
Federal Express
World On Time

"A lot of employees have built relationships with each other that will last the rest of our lives, and it's because this company promoted it. We get ticked off at each other, but it's like getting ticked off at your sister. You know you still love her."

Honi Reisman, Senior Manager, FedEx World Service Center

Courier Marty Herrera
Santa Fe, New Mexico

themselves usually make the most understanding, respected managers. Employees who step up to management complete a tough Leadership Evaluation and Awareness Process (LEAP), which emphasizes courage, dependability, judgment, integrity, empathy and charisma. In one five-year period, employees were promoted to manager from such job groups as ramp agents (344), mechanics (72), dispatchers (116), couriers/drivers (1,691), checker/sorters (262) and package handlers (114).

One of the best advertisements for the FedEx promote-from-within policy is Dave Rebholz, who started as a part-time clerk in Milwaukee, Wisconsin, in 1976. "I was the guy who washed trucks and ran packages out to the plane," he says. He also possessed a quality highly valued at FedEx: an eagerness to pitch in and get the task done, no matter whether it fit his job description. His enthusiasm and can-do pragmatism won him notice from managers, and Rebholz raced up the company structure, working in several divisions along the way. He is now senior vice-president of U.S. (Ground Operations), and he's sure it doesn't hurt him with the 60,000 people he manages that he's probably done their jobs at one time or another. "I've been in their shoes," Rebholz says. "It gives me a better opportunity to consider their views when making a decision."

Laurie Tucker started in finance in 1978. A resourceful, enthusiastic achiever who loves a challenge, Tucker earned an M.B.A. courtesy of FedEx. As senior vice-president of the Logistics, Electronic Commerce and Catalog division, she now manages 2,000 people and is proud that as she moved up in the company, many of those who worked for her are now FedEx vice-presidents. Two of the three years in which she was honored with the company's highest achievement award, the Five Star, were the years she gave birth to her two children. "That shows me that this is

28

When the name Federal Express was chosen in the early 1970s, it suited the company's scope, which was confined to the United States. Over 25 years, the company's customer base, geographic reach and service offerings evolved dramatically. In time, "FedEx" became a synonym around the world for "get it there fast."

After months of research with employees, customers and business leaders worldwide, the ever-entrepreneurial company made a bold change, shortening its brand name to FedEx. Employees gathered in a Memphis hangar to celebrate the vibrant new identity on June 24, 1994.

a company that measures results not on whether you are male or female, but on what you accomplish," she says.

Indeed, just as FedEx shipments are treated equally — each is a "golden package" — so, too, are FedEx employees. This approach stems from the deeply ingrained desire to treat employees, all employees, with respect. "As a global enterprise, FedEx embraces and reflects the diversity of the communities we serve," says James A. Perkins, senior vice-president and chief personnel officer. "The FedEx culture fosters an environment where a person's performance is what counts. We look at whether someone is producing, getting results, not at that person's color or sex. We're always looking for the best talent out there — period."

Sharon Hawkins agrees. "I knew when I got into FedEx that my opportunities were unlimited. It was up to me," says the senior personnel system specialist, who started in data entry in 1979 at age 21 and has since won two Five Star Awards.

"FedEx has always been open to female leadership," says Paola High, an employee-relations adviser who has been with the company since 1978. "The opportunities have opened up even more due to training and some strong FedEx women." In fact, 27 percent of current management is made up of women. The company also has been recognized for its dedication to hiring and advancing minorities. Several times, *Hispanic* magazine cited FedEx as one of the top 100

The men and women of FedEx, it seems, like the challenge of working for the best. In January 1998, *Fortune* magazine ranked FedEx near the top of its "The 100 Best Companies to Work for in America," at an enviable No. 18. The survey praised FedEx for its extremely low turnover rate, its ability to create jobs and its commitment to maintaining those jobs. It also cited the FedEx jumpseat policy, calling it one of the "most unusual" benefits in American business.

VERMONT

WITH SMOKE OBSCURING THE HIGHWAY along his rural route near Williston, Vermont, courier Steve Kolinich guessed things had gotten out of hand for some farmer burning his field. So he stopped to offer help. Sure enough, a row of flames was nearing a farmhouse. Kolinich called his dispatcher to notify the fire department. Then Kolinich and the farmer grabbed a rake and shovel to beat back the fire until a fire truck arrived. • Never thinking of the danger to himself, Kolinich borrowed a firefighter's portable pack, strapped it on and helped hose down the blaze, saving several farm buildings. When the fire was extinguished, Kolinich continued his route. "I had to get going," he says. "I still had deliveries" — all of which he made on time. • Since then, Kolinich has joined the volunteer fire department. • STEVE KOLINICH, WITH FEDEX SINCE 1984

In each of the more than 210 countries where FedEx operates, the policy is to hire locally. Partly because it's the right thing to do. Partly because it's good business to have people on board who know the customers, speak the language, live the culture and understand the local business.

companies providing opportunities for Hispanics, and the magazine *Black Enterprise* has named

FedEx among the top 25 "Best Places for Blacks to Work."

The ultimate expression of the FedEx fairness-to-all doctrine is a grievance procedure called

Guaranteed Fair Treatment. This includes a hearing at the management level closest to the

employee and the opportunity for appeals up through the system. The Supreme Court of FedEx,

the Appeals Board, is staffed by senior executives and meets once a week. Fred Smith often

attends. It is unusual for leaders at any company to commit such a large chunk of time to see that

grievances are handled correctly, but executives see the appeals process as a means to identify and

correct trouble spots. If the Appeals Board reverses a lower decision, the case may be published

(without names) so managers can use the information in their decision-making.

But it is not just formalized policies that make a difference. When Smith was awarded the

prestigious Wright Brothers Memorial Trophy for excellence in aviation at a black-tie dinner in

Washington, D.C., in 1996, he brought along 12 employees from various divisions to represent

all FedEx people.

One of the company's best-loved programs is its christening of new planes. This is not a cham-

pagne-bottle-breaking event but rather a family occasion: The planes are named after

employees' children. To get a Mariah or an Alex painted near the cockpit window,

employees submit their child's name, and one is drawn from a basket each time a

new plane is added to the fleet.

GLOBAL OUTREACH FedEx is committed to another type of service,

one that has nothing to do with on-time delivery. Going hand in hand

During the 1991 Desert Shield/Desert Storm operation, FedEx flew 576 missions into Saudi Arabia, transporting one-third of the total cargo tonnage for the war effort. FedEx was the most active air-cargo participant in the Civilian Reserve Air Fleet.

31

FedEx has 143 women pilots
and 210 minority pilots, more
than many other airlines.
Here, Jimmy Gist and Ellen
Griffin confer.

with treating employees fairly is a strong sense of social responsibility — using FedEx resources to help those in need.

For example, FedEx maintains an alliance with the American Red Cross that combines the FedEx strength in overnight delivery with the Red Cross' strength in emergency relief. When disaster hits, FedEx ships out vital communications equipment that it stores at its Memphis hub. (After a hurricane ripped through the island of St. Croix in 1995, FedEx had satellite-communications equipment there within hours so the Red Cross could coordinate the shipment of food and supplies to the ravaged island.)

FedEx also aids families who have been separated by war or natural disaster. Through the Red Cross, FedEx ships critical relief supplies as well as documents and communiqués to trace relatives and bring families back together again. It amounts to hundreds of thousands of dollars worth of fast delivery contributed every year.

Since 1986 FedEx has sponsored the St. Jude Classic, a PGA event, raising more than $6.5 million for the St. Jude Children's Research Hospital in Memphis. FedEx contributed $1 million to the Library of Congress to create a digital repository online, and it transports medical

In fiscal 1997, FedEx invested $5.5 million in its U.S. employees through tuition reimbursement. The money helped 5,766 full-time and part-time employees further their education. Similar programs are in place for non-U.S. employees.

33

TRINIDAD

A freak storm inundated Port of Spain, the capital of Trinidad, just as then-customer service agent Steven De Freitas was getting the day's shipments ready for the shuttle to the airport. Stranded couriers started radioing in. One van had been submerged. The courier was safe, but there were pickups still to be made. • De Freitas headed out in another van and parked it on high ground. Then, wading through chest-high waters downtown, he collected the remaining packages from 15 to 20 customers. Holding them overhead, he got them back to the station in time for the shuttle. • It was all in a day's work for the island FedEx staff. "We were the only courier company out there," De Freitas says. "Everybody else had packed it in for the day." • STEVEN DE FREITAS, WITH FEDEX SINCE 1991

The global perspective that drives FedEx extends beyond the world of commerce. Since 1995, FedEx has transported more than $30 million worth of medical supplies and humanitarian relief to India, China and Vietnam. Within their own communities, FedEx employees contribute 100,000 volunteer hours every year.

supplies and aircraft parts for Orbis International, which operates a flying hospital where ophthalmologists teach surgical skills to doctors in developing countries.

FedEx also teamed up with Heart to Heart, which transports medical supplies to hospitals and clinics in developing countries. FedEx has flown three missions — to Vietnam, China and India, which included Mother Teresa's hospital in Calcutta. Couriers and agents in London, where the Heart to Heart shipment to Calcutta was staged, learned that toys were so scarce at one of Mother Teresa's orphanages that three stuffed animals were kept in a glass case to be looked at but not touched. The employees collected 10,000 stuffed animals and packed them in the belly of the MD-11. Surely it was the happiest cargo that plane ever carried.

Other employees demonstrate the same spirit of service. When floods hit North Dakota in the spring of 1997, three FedEx drivers in Omaha, Nebraska, volunteered to carry 121,000 pounds of food, clothing and cleaning supplies donated by Omaha citizens to the North Dakota town of Devils Lake. In 1995, FedEx pilots based in Anchorage donated more than $25,000 for materials for a Habitat for Humanity house and hundreds of hours to build it.

Another program, Adopt-a-School, is expanding across the FedEx network. Here, employees lend expertise and act as mentors to students at schools in their communities.

"Those two hours a week let me spend time with the kids during school hours," says Gladstone Wade, a network engineer who mentors at Memphis' Booker T. Washington High School. "It shows that the FedEx people policy doesn't just mean people extending to people in the company. It also means people extending to others outside the company."

"Dost thou love life? Then do not squander time, for that is the stuff life is made of."

BENJAMIN FRANKLIN

In its role as global corporate citizen, FedEx delivered tons of toys to one of Mother Teresa's orphanages in Calcutta, India.

Courier Evelyn Rodriguez
San Juan, Puerto Rico

The American Red Cross and FedEx: A Tradition of Teamwork

By Elizabeth Dole

 In one terrifying moment, a fire, tornado, hurricane, flood or other disaster can destroy a home, change a life or devastate a family. Victims of more than 68,000 disasters turn to the American Red Cross each year for shelter, meals and help getting back on their feet.

"Help Can't Wait" is a slogan we take seriously at the American Red Cross. We must be ready whenever and wherever people urgently need our help. Our 1.3 million volunteers make that response possible — as does our alliance with Federal Express and other corporations that share our commitment to community service.

At the Red Cross, we depend on people who have the know-how, the resources and the manpower to help us get the job done, even under the most challenging conditions. When record floods inundated Northern California in January 1997, thousands of families were forced from their homes. Ben Pierce, a Red Cross procurement specialist, was one of the first on the scene.

"Timing was critical," Ben said. "FedEx shipped our disaster equipment — including computers, printers and communication hardware such as phones, pagers and satellite units — so that it arrived within 24 hours. Thanks to their prompt and professional response, we could do a better job serving those affected by the flooding."

When the floods receded, FedEx employees returned to pack, ship and store Red Cross emergency equipment at corporate headquarters in Tennessee to be used when the next disaster strikes. It's a system that has functioned effectively and efficiently for hundreds of major disaster operations.

Due in large part to the example set by Federal Express, in-kind donations to the Red Cross have more than doubled over the past two fiscal years and now total over $11 million.

Fortunately for us all, such businesses recognize that we all have a stake in healthy communities. As individuals and institutions, we share responsibility for meeting the urgent needs of our neighbors, for enriching the lives of children, and for improving the quality of our lives. Thus community involvement — through charitable giving, blood drive sponsorship, paid time off for volunteering, loaned executives and donations of products and services — is a long-term investment, compatible with the interests of stockholders, employees and customers. And it's the right thing to do.

Congratulations to Federal Express — the men and women who sort packages, fly delivery planes and drive trucks, and keep the system running efficiently — on 25 years of exemplary service to their customers, and to their communities.

As President of the American Red Cross, Elizabeth Dole oversees nearly 30,000 staff and more than 1.3 million volunteers who comprise the world's foremost humanitarian organization and supplier of half of America's blood supply. Mrs. Dole served as U.S. Secretary of Transportation from 1983 to 1987 and as U.S. Secretary of Labor from 1989 to 1990.

THE 12 MEMPHIS SUPERHUB EMPLOYEES were stymied. There had to be a way to improve the minisort, the back-up procedure to handle any packages that are misdirected by earlier sorting or incorrectly addressed. Weekly for five months the employees met on the job. They met Saturdays. They met on their own time, over breakfasts that sometimes stretched into afternoon.

Their zeal led to a simple yet resourceful strategy to hang clearer signs to avoid misrouting, reorganize the staff, and appoint someone to direct the tractors taking shipments to the planes. The team's efforts saved FedEx nearly $1 million over 18 months and earned it the 1992 Rochester Institute of Technology/USA TODAY Quality Cup in the service category, an award that recognizes efforts made by U.S. companies to better their operations.

There's no company more passionate about bettering its operations than FedEx. Ten may be the level of perfection in gymnastics. In the Electoral College, 270 is the magic number that decides U.S. presidential elections. But at FedEx the figure that is obsessed over and strived for companywide is 100. As in 100 percent. As in flawless.

There is a name for this mad push for infallibility. And that is quality. Lots of companies like to throw the word around and talk endlessly about what it means. But it's pretty simple. It essentially means three things: Improve service, improve efficiency, improve satisfaction. Even before the word began appearing — with a capital Q — in business journals and seminars, FedEx was practicing the concept. It's what differentiated the upstart company from the competition. And through its history, quality is what has always given FedEx the edge as other companies have adopted ideas — from the money-back guarantee to tracking — that were pioneered by FedEx. At FedEx everyone — VPs, ramp agents, mechanics and meteorologists — is expected to join in

Couriers Jesse Moreno (left)
and Joseph Chavez
Sunnyvale, California

"At Federal Express the systems infrastructure has the effect of putting its own people in charge of the company. Behind that lies a philosophy that says: people first."

ROBERT H. WATERMAN JR.

The world's largest fleet of all-cargo aircraft boasts one of the industry's most enviable records for service reliability. Here, mechanics tend to maintenance at the Subic Bay hub.

the pursuit of quality, not as an extracurricular activity but as a bold-faced part of the job description. That's why FedEx emphasizes that its people are a key part of the quality picture. Employees who are happy and secure in their jobs take pride in doing them even better. This empowerment results in a corporate culture that gives permission to think beyond the parameters of the job.

Growth and change are not only expected at FedEx, they are mandated. The company expects people to anticipate customers' needs, to think of new services or refinements that will make customers' lives easier. No one asked FedEx to offer customers the ability to track package status or request courier pickups on the Internet. FedEx thought of these in 1994, before any other World Wide Web pages allowed users to do much of anything besides browse, and before any customers realized how valuable and time-saving such features would be.

Three times a year, FedEx sponsors a Quality Success Story program. FedEx Quality Action Teams from around the world submit their stories, documenting how they were able to improve service and efficiency and reduce costs. Teams have been acclaimed for such things as building more efficient boxes, speeding up customs-clearance time in England and compiling a list of conventions in New Orleans so that employees could anticipate volume surges and reduce delays.

FedEx has a group devoted to nothing but the pursuit of quality. The Quality and Process Improvement area, along with the Service Assurance Board Network, advises folks at every level of the company on how they can improve their operations. There is one area FedEx still hasn't conquered, however. "No one has figured out yet how to improve the weather," says Holly Threat, managing director of the group. (But FedEx does everything possible to prepare for Mother Nature's onslaughts: Even during summer, crews conduct drills to de-ice planes.

Well before national noise legislation required quieter airplanes, FedEx partnered with Pratt & Whitney to develop technology to reduce noise from its fleet of Boeing 727s. Many major airlines with 727s now benefit from FedEx's effort, producing quieter neighborhood skies everywhere.

41

And when rain or snow backs up air traffic, FedEx's advanced technology helps optimize flight patterns so that the planes with the biggest loads land first.)

The company takes quality seriously because at FedEx — in such a competitive industry and with a public image so closely identified with the two words "absolutely, positively" — anything less than 100 percent isn't good enough. With more than 3 million packages speeding their way through the system each night, even a 1 percent failure rate would mean 30,000 packages were missed — an absolutely, positively unacceptable number.

THE MEASURE OF SERVICE   Though it makes every effort to minimize service failures, FedEx has zero tolerance for disappointing customers. That's why it created the Service Quality Index. Using data captured by the FedEx information network, it assigns points to problems that can occasionally occur, such as late packages, invoice adjustments or missing proof of delivery.

To make sure the company stays vigilant, a team of senior executives meets once a week to scrutinize trends and service shortfalls from the previous week. This group focuses not on how well the planes, vans and workers did their jobs to deliver millions of shipments on time. Instead, it is consumed by finding ways all the work can be done better. At one meeting, the topic was why a replacement part wasn't available for a certain airplane. When was the problem detected? Why wasn't it detected earlier? How can we be sure this won't happen again? Since the weekly meeting was initiated in 1994, the frequency of service failures has decreased each year.

FedEx lives by the adage, you can't manage what you can't measure. And unlike companies that measure only financial performance, FedEx has systems to gauge improvement in all three aspects of the People-Service-Profit philosophy. The numbers are relentlessly tracked to make sure

Courier Phil Burque
San Francisco, California

the company is living up to its goals.

On the service side, the company talks to approximately 150,000 customers per year about their needs and how FedEx can better address them. Direct-mail surveys go to 7,600 of the largest customers. At random, customers who get help from a Customer Service Representative at 1•800•Go•FedEx® are later called by an outside organization to learn how the representative performed in such areas as courtesy, knowledge and empathy.

At FedEx, the pursuit and measurement of quality translate into better service in myriad ways. For instance, in 1988 customers said in surveys that they wanted the choice of an afternoon delivery at a lower price; FedEx introduced FedEx Standard Overnight®. And FedEx developed software that brings the caller's account profile to the Customer Service Representative's screen just seconds after the caller is done dialing, so customers can save time and get a personal greeting.

The FedEx passion for quality hasn't gone unnoticed. In 1990, FedEx won the Malcolm Baldrige National Quality Award — the first to win in the service category. In 1994, FedEx became the only global express transportation company to earn systemwide certification to the ISO 9001 international quality standard; in 1997, FedEx won recertification. Most companies register individual sites, but FedEx again set the pace by using technology and central control systems to gain registration of its entire worldwide network.

MINSK

MILWAUKEE

43

RETURNING FROM HIS DAILY COURIER ROUTE

in Bakersfield, California, Ed Cadena spotted a package that had missed the shuttle to Los Angeles. Despite having put in a full day, he loaded up the package and drove the four-hour round trip to the airport himself. "A customer hands us a package and expects it to be there the next day," says Cadena. • But that isn't the only way Cadena puts himself out for others. Each summer for 23 years, he has spent two weeks counseling at-risk kids at a camp in Sequoia National Forest. He typifies many FedEx people in his role as unofficial troop leader at the Bakersfield FedEx station. He makes sure coworkers are recognized, whether it is buying flowers for someone's ailing mother or posting pictures from a coworker's wedding. "It gives me a good feeling," he says. • ED CADENA, WITH FEDEX SINCE 1985

Courier Nancy Timpson
Toronto, Canada

HOUSTON ●

KUALA LUMPUR ●

46

Baldrige Award winners are called upon to share their knowledge in the year following their win. But FedEx was so enthusiastic about passing on the quality message that it began holding two dozen Quality Forums every year. Companies (73 of them in 1997) send people to Memphis from as far away as Norway and Japan to tour the SuperHub and learn from the FedEx model.

"We were impressed with the whole climate toward customer service," says Allen Rosen, whose FedEx visit was part of his mission to improve customer service at Union Camp, a paper products manufacturer based in Wayne, New Jersey. "We noticed that the attitude of doing whatever it takes to serve the customer came from the top down." Rosen took home FedEx's idea of training representatives extensively before they interact with customers on the phone.

If anything, the drive for quality is stronger now at FedEx than when it won the Baldrige Award. "It was one thing to be obsessed about quality when we were the only one in the market offering service backed by a money-back guarantee," Holly Threat says. "But over the years we've continually had to stay ahead of our competitors by creating new, better, faster services and tools for our customers to use."

For example, in 1995, FedEx gave customers an 8 a.m. next-business-day delivery commitment in nearly 5,000 U.S. ZIP codes with FedEx First Overnight®. In 1997, it introduced an unparalleled level of service that permits shipments from throughout Asia to arrive in the United States by 10:30 a.m. the next business day.

Because FedEx knows it must always stay one step ahead, it is constantly searching for ideas that will provide the most reliable, innovative service available anywhere. Every morning of every business day of every week of every month, the pressure is on to top yesterday. But no company performs better under pressure than FedEx.

FedEx Call Centers, including this one in Memphis, respond to more than 600,000 customer inquiries each business day.

In as few as 17 minutes, a FedEx ground crew empties a fully loaded plane. Theirs is the first act in a package-sorting ballet that occurs each night at FedEx hubs around the globe.

Checker/sorter Marcus Tolibas
Oakland, California

Going Above and Beyond

By Senator Ernest F. Hollings

I believe the astounding success Federal Express has achieved over the past 25 years can be attributed to three qualities: pioneering spirit, visionary leadership and business acumen. Certainly, these are qualities Fred Smith has in abundance. But to me, it's a greater credit to Fred that these have become characteristics shared by FedEx employees around the world.

Thanks to Fred's leadership, there is a cultural commitment to exceptional service among FedEx employees that sets the company apart. While FedEx is blessed with a talented team of executives, managers, pilots and couriers, it is their dedication and hard work that have led to the company's phenomenal growth.

From FedEx's early beginnings as no more than an idea on a college economics paper to its worldwide leadership in express transportation, FedEx operations have been marked by persistence.

Yet, to me, the company's greatest successes have come in the form of assistance to its neighbors. In keeping with Fred's training as a U.S. Marine, FedEx has gone above and beyond the call of duty in providing humanitarian aid countless times. Neither I, nor the farmers of South Carolina, will ever forget that when the state was stricken with drought, FedEx put one of its jets at my disposal to ferry hay to feed our livestock. This averted economic disaster for South Carolina.

For its success in the business world, FedEx has earned my respect; for its philanthropy, it has earned my admiration. I am delighted to congratulate FedEx on 25 years of unrivaled achievements and extend my wishes for continued success in the 21st century.

Ernest F. Hollings was first elected to the U.S. Senate in 1966. He represents the state of South Carolina.

49

BUILDING THE NETWORK

Fred Smith piloted his twin passions for aviation and transportation into what early FedEx ads hailed as America's new airline.

IN 1971, A MAN named Ted Weise, formerly with a commuter airline in Memphis, Tennessee, made a call to Little Rock, Arkansas, in search of a job. He spoke with Fred Smith, owner of Arkansas Aviation, which dealt in corporate jets. Smith was rumored to be starting some kind of new airline. Smith said he was not quite ready to hire anyone but that Weise should keep in touch.

When Weise finally landed an interview, Smith asked why he wanted to work for Federal Express, the new airline. "I said I liked working with planes," recalls Weise, now president and chief executive officer of FedEx, "but he didn't particularly like that answer." Smith explained that he needed employees with passion, energy and a determination to work hard. Weise declared that he had those qualities, and Smith hired him.

During that interview, Weise found out that this new airline was unusual, to say the least. It was not about the romance of air travel, since its aim was to move packages, not people. Nor was it about transporting packages in the usual way, in the bellies of passenger airliners. Federal Express had a startling and revolutionary new concept — to devote a fleet of jets to the overnight delivery of packages, and to gather together a unique team of people in pursuit of the goal of providing the highest quality service. Later Smith would encapsulate this mission simply as "People-Service-Profit."

Smith, a Mississippi native who learned to fly at age 15, came from a family of transportation entrepreneurs that included a riverboat pilot and the founder of a successful interstate bus line. As a U.S. Marine he flew 230 combat missions in Vietnam, and his harsh wartime experience gave him the desire to immerse himself in productive and rewarding activities. He acquired Arkansas Aviation in 1969, but his ultimate goal was to apply his energy to something more

world-changing than the sale of aircraft.

As a political science and economics student at Yale, Smith had written a paper on the logistical challenges facing pioneering firms in the information-technology industry. He saw that no company could afford to keep a full inventory of spare parts for computers and other data-processing machines. Yet as computers became more common, businesses grew reliant upon them and vulnerable to the havoc that an idle machine could cause. Smith concluded that a new system to move parts quickly, overnight and door-to-door, had to replace physical inventories.

Perhaps Smith's professor didn't recognize the revolutionary implications of his student's thesis; in any event, the paper received only an average grade. But the budding entrepreneur was not deterred. Smith wanted to start the world's first airline that would reliably meet the needs of the growing numbers of companies in desperate and immediate need of parts. For these firms, "ASAP," "next week" or "some time" were just not fast enough.

Reliability and speed had never been strengths of existing air-cargo services, which commonly consigned their customers' shipments to the bellies of passenger planes. Because passenger airlines scheduled most of their flights during the day, when it was most convenient for travelers, next-day delivery was rare. In addition, service to areas outside the largest cities required many transfers or was simply not available.

Smith concluded that Federal Express — a name chosen for its patriotic ring, its implication of national scope and hoped-for business from the Federal Reserve Bank — could streamline operations by using a hub-and-spoke method of distribution, where all packages arrived at a central point for sorting, then were reloaded onto planes and flown to their destinations. He hit upon this tactic by observing how the banking industry collected canceled checks at a central sorting location and distributed them to individual banks.

The first Drop Boxes hit street corners in 1975. Today customers have more than 40,000 places to drop off shipments.

In 1971, when Smith was just 27, he incorporated Federal Express and sought investors. All found the idea brazen. Many did not think the plan of using a single city as a "hub" would work, and some doubted the need for an overnight delivery service. To sway the latter group, Smith hired two firms to study the business plan and research the potential customer base. Both reported that Federal Express could find a large and welcoming market. In fact, they said, transporting air freight in the United States represented more than $1 billion in annual business.

Smith put up $4 million of his own money, and investors eventually kicked in another $80 million. At last Smith could begin hiring a skeleton staff — many of them former members of the military, such as executive vice-president Irby Tedder, who had been a deputy wing commander in the Strategic Air Command.

By this time, in 1972, visitors to Federal Express headquarters in Little Rock saw a striking scene. In selecting the "minifreighter" for its fleet, the company had settled upon the Dassault Falcon, a French-made corporate jet. Federal Express bought 33 of them, eight used and 25 new, many of which had sat for two years in the New Mexico desert awaiting a buyer. With modifications, the Falcon could carry 6,500 pounds over a range of 1,400 to 1,800 miles. Inside the hangar, workers swarmed around the Falcons, gutting the passenger cabins. They ripped out passenger doors, replacing them with five-by-six-foot cargo doors, and painted the planes vivid shades of purple and orange. Some mechanics worked 48 straight days, without a day off, to make the needed modifications. A sofa in the hangar served double duty as a bed. No one thought any of this was strange. It was exhilarating — and necessary as the first steps toward creating an airline that would change the world.

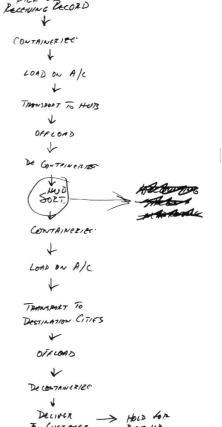

55

Signs of genius: An early diagram of the hub-and-spoke concept, copied by other carriers.

"As long as every competitor marches to the same

beat, speed isn't necessary. It becomes a competitive

requirement when someone marches faster and they are

rewarded for it. Such is the Federal Express story."

CHRISTOPHER MEYER, FAST CYCLE TIME

People in the office also threw themselves into readying the Falcon fleet. Claudia Betzner had been hired in April 1972 as a charter coordinator, but she spent her first day on the job photo-copying pilot-training documents. "Some nine hours later I thought, 'What have I gotten myself into?'" she recalled.

All this time, Federal Express had been negotiating with airport authorities in Little Rock about establishing the company's home base there. The city, after all, had a good central location. All the airport needed were some new facilities for FedEx. Like many investors, however, airport managers in Little Rock saw little reason to risk millions of dollars to support a fledgling airline that had not yet delivered an overnight package, might never make a profit, and could sink into bankruptcy.

Memphis, Tennessee, had different ideas. That city's entrepreneurial airport authorities already had some old Air National Guard hangars available for Federal Express at the edge of their land, reducing by half the amount of financing Federal Express needed. Might this overnight delivery idea, they wondered, bring Memphis new jobs, keep the airport busy at night and make the city a shipping center? Memphis made the bet, and in March 1973 Federal Express moved its Airline Operations Department there, with the rest of the company soon to follow.

Sky's the Limit Federal Express had built its business plan, assembled its fleet, hired its staff, set up sorting facilities in the old hangars and even rounded up some contract work — the delivery of airmail for the U.S. Postal Service — but as yet no overnight packages had been delivered. Employees were eager to see the system working. So on a March night in 1973, FedEx tested its unique express-delivery concept. Twelve cities in the East and Midwest were the initial

LITTLE ROCK, FEBRUARY 1973 – "It was 7 a.m., and I was just finishing about my 12th cup of coffee for the night when this guy came out of his office. He looked as though it had been more than a few nights since he'd seen a genuine bed and flopped down beside me. We talked about our respective nights' work, problems out in the field, and just where we thought all this chaos would lead. Suddenly, this belea-guered guy got wide awake, looked me square in the eye and said, 'Bob, the day is coming when you'll see a DC-10 parked outside this door, your flight plans and weather will be computerized, and your biggest decision before you taxi out will be whether you want your cof-fee black or with cream and sugar.' This guy with the tousled hair, wrinkled shirt and scuffed shoes was — you got it — Fred Smith."

MD-11 SENIOR CAPTAIN ROBERT DUFRESNE, BASED IN ANCHORAGE, ALASKA

markets, and a small sales staff labored to establish accounts in those places. A squadron of Falcons awaited the packages, with couriers primed to pick up and deliver them in cars and vans.

When the sun rose after that long-anticipated night, only seven packages had been received into the FedEx system, fewer than one for each plane Federal Express owned. They all were delivered overnight, but Ted Weise remembers that employees "could have done the sorting in the trunk of a car." Back to the drawing board.

The people of Federal Express reexamined their strategy with characteristic energy and creativity. Twelve cities obviously had not been enough to make a go of it, and more were added to the system. The company also better defined its levels of service, including: Priority One, offering door-to-door delivery by noon the next business day; and Economy Air, providing door-to-door service on the second business day.

On April 17, 1973, Federal Express felt ready to activate the system once again for overnight deliveries. The network now included 25 U.S. cities (and a radius of 25 miles around them), from Boston to Cleveland to Minneapolis. Fourteen Falcons were fueled and readied. Sales reps, pilots, ground crew, package sorters, couriers — 389 employees in all — eagerly awaited the day's volume count.

By the end of that momentous evening, more than seven packages had arrived at the hub in Memphis. Many more. The package total that night was 186, and FedEx has been delivering express packages continuously ever since. Fred Smith's vision — to efficiently merge the aviation and package delivery businesses, creatively blending resources and skills in a way America had never before seen — had taken shape. The company was shaking on its legs like a newborn colt, but it had arisen, thanks to the energy of the FedEx people.

In those very first weeks in April 1973 when the FedEx network was launched for good, employees learned as they worked, and they worked hard. In some cities the pilots loaded packages onto the Falcons. Station managers and couriers often used their own cars for deliveries. One part-time courier, Gary Bockelman, became an instant hero for pawning his wristwatch on his first night on the job in order to buy fuel for his delivery van. Employees at the FedEx Philadelphia office worked from a corner of the pilot's lounge of another airline, and the Pittsburgh office conducted its business from a motel room. Whenever the flow of packages overwhelmed the resources of the Memphis sorting hub, Federal Express people streamed from their offices to help out.

During the first year of overnight delivery, the company's workforce more than tripled to 1,100. Package volume topped 1,000 per night, then exceeded 1,500. The Falcons became a familiar sight in the Tennessee skies. But this growth did not bring financial stability. Toward the end of 1973, Federal Express fell behind in paying its bills. Though it had been the most heavily financed start-up in U.S. transportation history, the company needed still more money to expand the network to new cities, enlarge the workforce and maintain the planes. On November 13,

Secretary Sherry Lynne Rowland Little, who joined FedEx on February 5, 1973, has badge No. 268.

59

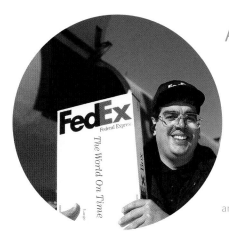

A PLANE BOUND FOR NEWARK, NEW JERSEY, from Manchester, New Hampshire, had spilled hydraulic fluid on takeoff and returned to the gate. Hall Hoover, who services ground equipment, was part of the crew taking care of the spill. An aircraft mechanic located the problem — a broken fitting in the hydraulic feed line. A second plane was sent from Newark to bring a new part and pick up the freight. But the cargo couldn't be transferred to the spare plane because the hydraulic problem kept the main cargo door on the disabled plane from opening. • It looked as if the freight would remain on the ground overnight. But Hoover had an idea. He found a ball bearing from a diesel engine and inserted it into the hydraulic fitting to plug the leak. This created enough pressure to open the door. The freight was transferred, and the plane got back to Newark in time for the next day's deliveries. • HALL HOOVER, WITH FEDEX SINCE 1987

1973, the crisis ended when investors agreed to extend FedEx another $52 million in financing.

Just over a year later, in February 1975, FedEx turned its first monthly profit, $20,000. This ended a two-year streak during which FedEx averaged monthly losses of more than $1 million.

Financial pressures did not tempt Federal Express to alter its famous business mission, "People-Service-Profit." By treating employees well and emphasizing the highest levels of service, Smith believed, profits would eventually follow. The company used a good deal of its financial resources to further nurture the FedEx strategy of service, and it put more money to work in developing exemplary employment practices. The company established, for instance, a kind of bill of rights for its workers, complete with job-security provisions, fair and standard procedures for dealing with complaints, a peer-review board and strong promotion opportunities.

In typically bold style, Federal Express also reached out to potential customers. Up until 1975, conventional cargo carriers rarely advertised outside of professional or trade publications. But Federal Express was not your typical shipping company, and it had big plans for taking shipping decisions to the front offices, not just the docks. That meant spending $350,000 in 1975 to advertise in consumer magazines and, even more unconventionally, on television. "America, you've got a new airline," the commercials proclaimed. Only this new breed of airline transported packages, not people, with its own fleet.

The results were gratifying. Daily package volume climbed to 13,500 by the end of 1975, and the year's revenues reached $60 million. The next year, those figures rose to 19,000 packages and $96 million, with service to 75 cities.

Predictions of doom, such as *Business Week*'s 1974 forecast that Federal Express could not possibly continue its growth, became faint memories.

LOS ANGELES

CHARLOTTE

The Falcon was so small, it could fit in a DC-10's tail. By mid-1975, Falcons like "Lisa" could not keep up with the surging demand for express service.

At age 32, Fred Smith shows his grit before Congress. His request, says FDX Executive Vice President Ken Masterson, was as bold and unthinkable as wanting to change the Internal Revenue Code.

THE FIGHT FOR SURVIVAL Everyone at FedEx could see, in fact, that the potential for future growth was huge and that only the limited load capacity of the Falcons was slowing things down. In September 1975, the company formally requested the Civil Aeronautics Board (CAB), the federal agency that oversaw the airline industry, to allow Federal Express to acquire and operate five larger-capacity jet aircraft, which would give the company payloads of up to 15,000 pounds and save fuel. The CAB rejected this request, citing an existing law that prevented air-taxi services from operating aircraft with a load capacity greater than 7,500 pounds. That law, however, had been enacted with passenger airlines in mind, not freight carriers.

Federal Express suddenly found itself in the position of having to lobby the government for its survival. Without a change in the airline-regulation laws, the company could never become more than a niche player in the shipping business. FedEx wanted to provide overnight service for customers beyond the largest metropolitan areas, lower its rates and expand its network. The ability to fly larger cargo planes was imperative. The way FedEx saw it, the law had to be changed.

The company urged employees to write their Congressional representatives in support of deregulation legislation. "Let's get those letters to Congress now.... Our future depends on it," one 1976 memo to employees declared. Fred Smith encamped in Washington. Despite these efforts — and faced with rigorous opposition by a large air-cargo carrier and others — Congress decided not to allow the exemption for larger aircraft.

The next year, Federal Express led an even more determined effort to eliminate all economic regulation of air-cargo operations, which it believed harmed the interests of carriers and the public. The company spearheaded an effective lobbying committee comprised of other freight

Federal Express

EIGHT MASSIVE WINDOWS HAD TOPPLED INSIDE A TRUCK at a hotel loading dock, trapping a laborer underneath. "The truck was so big that you could hear the howls but couldn't tell where they were coming from," says Bobby Brown, who had driven up to deliver shipments at the same loading dock. • Brown and others scrambled into the truck and tried to lift the windows off the man, but they were too heavy. Then Brown warned everybody to move, positioned himself under the load and shoved with all his might. Amid the cheers of bystanders, the victim was able to crawl to safety. "Something just told me I had to do something or watch a person die," Brown says. "I'd want somebody to take that risk for me." • The man said Brown had saved his life. But despite some glass splinters in his back that were discovered days later, Brown simply resumed his route. • **BOBBY BROWN, WITH FEDEX SINCE 1989**

carriers and commuter airlines. Federal Express worked diligently to explain to members of Congress and President Jimmy Carter's staff the need to remove regulations that forced FedEx to fly several Falcons at a time between Memphis and New York or Chicago instead of sending one large plane. FedEx employees were dispatched to the U.S. Capitol to give testimony. As Smith explained to members of the House of Representatives' Aviation Subcommittee, "Federal Express has managed to survive and grow, and to provide an exceptionally valuable and needed public service, in spite of existing federal regulation, not because of it."

FedEx's prosperity was living proof of the need for improved domestic shipping service. "FedEx made deregulation into a consumer issue, explaining that these regulations cost every family in the U.S. $250 a year because they were indirectly paying for industry's inventory maintenance and excess equipment," says Robert Delaney, executive vice-president of Cass Information Systems, North America's largest provider of information services and systems to the logistics and transportation industry. "You could already see that FedEx was creating a time-critical shipment industry."

President Carter placed his weight behind the effort, and on November 7, 1977, he signed Public Law 95-163. At last Federal Express could use larger aircraft, schedule them on routes without geographic restrictions and set prices to match market

63

"Some of the early service centers were just counters in front of someone else's lobby," says Steve Kastens, a counter agent since 1982. "We'd walk out to street corners and hand out pins to drum up business."

demand. Without the determination of FedEx people, however, America might have been stuck in the distribution "dark ages" for many years to come.

FedEx old-timers still recall the party that erupted after the deregulation victory, in a bar near the company's Memphis headquarters. "It was a real high-energy get-together, with guys cutting their ties off and tacking them to the walls," one employee remembers. "It was one of our big turning points."

Federal Express promptly closed a deal to buy seven Boeing 727s from United Airlines for $26 million. Each had a cargo capacity of 40,000 pounds — seven times the load of a Falcon — and would begin flying in January 1978. "We all sobered up quickly after that," Ted Weise says. "We had to work on getting those 727s on line. They would certainly put us in a different league and along a new path. We all understood the enormity of this change."

"With the christening of our first 727s, we saw the end of an era at Federal Express," Smith said at the time, "the closing of a period when company legends were made — fun to remember and hell to repeat. The stranglehold the government regulations placed on our ability to develop and grow is gone. Now we face new challenges, unlimited opportunities, and an exciting future."

With the help of these new airplanes, Federal Express ended the 1970s as a company in some ways much different from the start-up that had spread its wings in 1973. The company's shares were now publicly traded on the New York Stock Exchange, and FedEx had launched its first international services, into Canada. By 1979, the FedEx fleet numbered 1,454 vans, 12 Boeing 727s, four Boeing 737s, 32 faithful Falcons and 39 other aircraft on lease. FedEx offered direct overnight service to twice as many U.S. domestic destinations as its competitors. Incredibly, Federal Express was now the nation's leading air-cargo carrier, with a daily volume of 100,000 packages within reach.

CHICAGO
MONACO

Package-filled containers (curved to fit snugly inside aircraft) zipped across the tarmac at FedEx hubs.

As this 1988 photo shows, information technology is as integral to FedEx as planes, people and packages. FedEx operates one of the world's busiest data-processing centers, daily handling more than 60 million information requests from more than 3,000 databases and more than 500,000 archive files.

FEDEX GREW SO REMARKABLY not only because of its determination to overcome obstacles, the simplicity of the "People-Service-Profit" philosophy and the hard work of its people, but also because right from the start the company was driven to harness information technology. The company's first computer, a Burroughs 1700, arrived in 1972. Six years later, when the daily volume stood at a modest 40,000 packages, FedEx had already invested in two large IBM mainframe computers that ran at just a fraction of their capacity. "That said to me, here's a company that understands the value of technology," says Winn Stephenson, corporate vice-president, FDX Information Systems, who started with FedEx in 1979 as manager of communications software.

A hallmark of the FedEx approach to technology was to play with it and never fear stretching it to the limit to serve customers better. For example, having radio contact with its fleet of vans and trucks was important, but Federal Express wanted a much higher level of communication — the digital transmission of data to in-vehicle terminals. When FedEx implemented the Digitally Assisted Dispatch System (DADS) in 1980, tiny terminals were installed in each vehicle, guiding couriers to their next pickup.

In its next big technological step, FedEx developed technology that could track the status of each package in its hands. Beginning in 1986, couriers and package sorters had their own bar-code scanners — the world's first use of bar-code technology to track package status in transit electronically — transforming FedEx employees into distribution processors and information gatherers. Few customers noticed. They only cared that their shipments arrived on time and that the rare misdirected package could be located and correctly routed in minutes.

Starting in 1987, Federal Express continued this technological innovation by giving high-

67

FedEx Commercials Make History In the belief that advertising plays an important role in reflecting – and creating – American culture, the National Museum of American History's Center for Advertising History in Washington, D.C., collects significant ad campaigns. Included in the collection: the "Absolutely, Positively Overnight" commercials, directed by advertising legend Joe Sedelmaier.

As Fred Smith told the archivists, "One of the reasons the 'Absolutely, Positively' campaign was so important was that it was a whole new generation of commercials. Nobody had ever done anything like it. It became almost a culture. People waited for the next commercial."

volume customers use of their own FedEx PowerShip® terminals. At a time when desktop computers were still uncommon and expensive, installing computers in customer offices seemed radical. But it proved visionary, as thousands of customers adopted them to process shipments fast and efficiently. Later, FedEx Ship® software turned customers' own computers into remote shipping stations capable of processing shipments, scheduling pickups, tracking package status and printing shipping labels. Eventually, FedEx would use its World Wide Web site to turn the Internet into everyman's shipping tool.

GOING ON THE AIR If FedEx earned customers' respect for its revolutionary use of technology during the late 1970s and 1980s, it riveted their attention through its surreal and funny advertising, the work of the firm Ally & Gargano. "These ads worked so well because they were on the cutting edge — they put onto the screen people everyone had met but had never before seen on TV," says Brian Fernee, president of the media management firm RNF Media, Inc., and an authority on television advertising. "They were unique because they grabbed your attention without being offensive." Whereas most companies aim for either increased business or fame with their advertising, FedEx ads delivered both.

1973
FedEx begins operations with service to 25 cities

1974
Volume reaches 10,000 packages per night

1975
Posts first profit

Installs first Drop Box

1976
Launches Standard Air Service

1977
Deregulation of air-cargo industry

1978
Delivery of first Boeing 727

1979
Offers first international service, to Canada

By 1980, the company's advertising budget had swelled to $10 million — 30 times what it had been five years earlier — and it would grow much larger. The company had learned that a high rate of repeat business made it economical to invest heavily in advertising that would attract new customers.

The first ads simply created awareness of the new company. Then followed a string of legendary campaigns, including the "Hellooooo, Federal" commercials in 1980 that showed how simple it was to arrange for pickups, and the "Why Fool Around with Anyone Else?" ads beginning in 1983 that touted the 10:30 a.m. commitment and other services. All took their cue from 1979's hugely successful "Absolutely, Positively Overnight" ads, which humorously depicted a cruel and unforgiving corporate world in which shippers lost sleep over the fate of their packages, bosses screamed and rapped the heads of employees when things went wrong, overextended workers routinely faced insane demands, and businesses could perish with the late arrival of a single package. Other campaigns featured a mile-a-minute talker, the benefits of tracking and the company's money-back guarantee — all to convince shippers they could trust FedEx for everyday needs, not just emergencies.

While these ads were establishing a witty, accessible and very human public personality for FedEx, they also announced the arrival of new FedEx services, which were needed to meet

FedEx operates one of the largest private mobile radio networks anywhere, with more than 45,000 wireless units. The network, called the Digitally Assisted Dispatch System (DADS), alerts FedEx couriers of pickups and enters package data into FedEx's tracking system.

69

1981
Opens Memphis SuperHub

Introduces Overnight Letter

1980
Implements DADS
(Digitally Assisted
Dispatch System)

1982
Offers first 10:30 a.m.
next-business-day commitment

1983
Becomes first U.S. company to
achieve revenues of $1 billion in
10 years without merger or acquisition

1984
Launches ZapMail

Launches international operations in
Europe and Asia/Pacific following
acquisition of Gelco Express International

1985
Establishes dedicated daily flights to Europe;
opens European headquarters in Brussels

Included in *The 100 Best Companies to
Work for in America*

customers' needs and keep the company ahead of a growing pack of competitors. The first addition of the 1980s was the Overnight Letter, which rolled out in 1981 when changes in U.S. postal regulations allowed private companies to deliver legal papers, blueprints and other documents. Most important, this new offering developed a market not in customers' warehouses or shipping departments but in their front offices. In the year it was introduced, the Overnight Letter brought in $56 million, achieved a daily volume of 27,000 pieces and greatly improved FedEx revenues per pound carried. Here was further proof that FedEx's vision matched the needs of its customers.

Another new service, ZapMail, did not succeed — yet it showed Federal Express in true form as an entrepreneurial, risk-taking company. Introduced in 1984 as a way to provide same-day delivery for document facsimiles, ZapMail linked the FedEx digital satellite communications network with its delivery network. These were the days before fax machines were common, and customers could use ZapMail's high-quality facsimile technology to deliver documents to recipients in two hours or less.

ZapMail appeared to be an ideal way to stretch the boundaries and raise the standards of rapid document delivery. Federal Express invested hundreds of millions of dollars to develop and market ZapMail, yet the idea never caught on among customers and was phased out in 1987. "We thought at the time that we could establish a new frontier," says FedEx board member

1986
Exceeds 1 million packages per night (December 22, with 1,018,299)

1987
Introduces FedEx PowerShip® automated shipping capability for customers

1988
Launches first direct scheduled service to Japan

1989
Completes operational merger of Flying Tigers

Introduces
FedEx International Priority®

1990
Receives Malcolm Baldrige National Quality Award, first to win in service category

Accepts delivery of first MD-11

Jackson W. Smart Jr., "but we didn't realize how fast the cost of fax machines would drop. We tried it, it didn't work, so we took our lumps and went away." The lesson learned was not to avoid risk — that would clash with FedEx's commitment to providing superior service — but to recognize that not every well-executed idea will be a winner. That was important wisdom for a company that had seemingly never before made a serious misstep.

Despite its eventual failure, ZapMail had other surprising benefits. Because at the time it was the only commercial service to deliver documents overnight from North America to Europe, it gave FedEx an early leg up in the transatlantic express business. And when the company closed down the service without laying off employees, FedEx people saw the truth of the "People-Service-Profit" commitment.

ZapMail represented only a small portion of FedEx revenues, and the rest of the company's operations continued to soar. Nowhere was this more evident than at the new and exciting sorting facility in Memphis, named the SuperHub, which symbolized the steady acceleration of business. Over time the SuperHub received numerous updates and expansions. For business was overwhelmingly good. In 1980, the first DC-10s came onboard, requiring 500 pounds of purple,

71

The FedEx SuperHub in Memphis covers 294 acres, within which snakes a 172-mile maze of conveyors, chutes and automatic sort belts. Expansion plans will put it at 439 acres by the year 2004.

FedEx
Federal Express
The World On Time®

1994
Launches "FedEx" as official brand name with slogan "The World On Time®"

Accepts delivery of first Airbus A-300 and A-310

Introduces FedEx Ship®, allowing customers to ship packages and track package status from their desktop computers

Receives simultaneous ISO 9001 certification for all worldwide operations

Launches World Wide Web home page, making FedEx one of the first businesses to offer online customer-service tools

1995
Acquires Evergreen International, with authority to serve China

Opens hub facility at Subic Bay, the Philippines

1996
Opens European hub at Charles de Gaulle Airport

Introduces FedEx interNetShip℠ to let customers process packages on the Internet

1997
Opens hub at Alliance Airport in Dallas-Ft. Worth, Texas

Announces distance-based pricing

Announces development of Miami hub to enhance service for Latin America and the Caribbean

TWO DAYS BEFORE CHRISTMAS 1996, Lissa Marshall got a call from a FedEx courier carrying the day's pickups from Moscow, Idaho. A traffic accident, exacerbated by snow and ice, had halted traffic on a straight stretch of road. The Idaho State Police refused to let anyone through. The courier would not make it back to Lewiston that afternoon in time for the outbound plane. • "We had time-sensitive shipments from the hospital and perishable packages from the University of Idaho," recalls Marshall, a senior service agent. "I thought, maybe if I call the police and tell them we have medical packages on board, they would let him by." • She explained the problem. The state patrol made no promises, but 15 minutes later Marshall had good news: The courier had been escorted past the accident scene and was on his way. When told she had saved the day, Marshall was astonished. "I was just doing my job," she says. • **LISSA MARSHALL, WITH FEDEX SINCE 1987**

orange and white paint to transform each one. In 1983, Federal Express became the first company in U.S. history to reach $1 billion in revenues in 10 years without acquiring another firm. The following year, FedEx hit the landmark of sorting 500,000 packages in a single night; the figure reached 1 million in 1986. Sales exceeded $2 billion in 1985, $3 billion in 1987 and $4 billion in 1989. By the end of the decade, FedEx service was available to 99 percent of the U.S. population.

Good as these times were, people at FedEx never stopped reexamining their strategies. Even the single-hub system — the pride of the FedEx distribution philosophy from its earliest days — came under scrutiny because the bigger FedEx grew, the more sense it made to add new hubs for increased flexibility, improved efficiency and earlier package delivery.

During the 1980s, Federal Express grew into a multi-billion-dollar company, yet it had not forgotten its past. Even as revenues mushroomed and markets multiplied, the little Dassault Falcon jet remained dear to the hearts of FedEx people. On August 30, 1983, FedEx Falcon 8FE, the company's very first jet, took to the air one last time. Employees volunteered their time and money to refurbish the craft — leaving their signatures and messages hidden behind panels — and Fred Smith piloted the Falcon on its final flight. Then the company donated the plane to the Smithsonian Institution. The next year, the last Falcon was retired from the FedEx fleet.

"Federal Express has been the epitome of excellence

in operation and excellence in innovation during the past

two decades, during which it completely redrew the

boundaries of the air cargo market."

AIR TRANSPORT WORLD

Courier Dam Lam Danh
Ho Chi Minh City, Vietnam

FedEx

By Tom Peters

It's a helluva note to write a valedictory to FedEx that starts with a UPS story. But I will. You see, I grew up in the 1950s, when Presidents of the United States were made or broken over strikes ... i.e., whether or not to stop a miners' strike ... or a railroad strike.

Even into the 1990s, modems and PCs and Web browsers notwithstanding, we still retained the railroad mindset. And then UPS went on strike in 1997. And AARP members' prescription drugs were not delivered. And thus we discovered that ... WE HAD ALL ARRIVED AT THE-AGE-OF-FEDEX. That is, the new world now depends on ... ABSOLUTELY, POSITIVELY OVERNIGHT. (I know that's an old FedEx slogan ... but it best describes the revolution.)

In August 1997 I gave a seminar in Zimbabwe. FedEx supported it. And I — inadvertently — supported FedEx. I said — in an uncompromising fashion — that Zimbabweans simply couldn't play the World-Class Game they want to play ... unless they play it The FedEx Way.

You see, I cofounded a textile company in 1996. Most of our production is in India and China. We recently got a big order from Neiman Marcus. (A breakthrough for us.) A hitch occurred here ... and a hitch occurred there. My command to my colleagues: "Ship it FedEx. Neiman's doesn't care if it's produced in Dallas or Delhi. They expect it ... on time ... all the time ... to the minute."

Well, I beat up my Indian colleagues ... and then my pals in Zimbabwe. I insisted: It's an on-time/all-the-time world. Period. Production in Delhi. Production in Harare. Or Bangkok. Or Monterrey. Or Santiago. No matter. No difference. That is: Good stuff. On time. All the time. No excuses.

The computer/information-systems revolution's impact on the factory, it turns out, has been marginal. The real information-systems revolution? Ask L.L. Bean. Or Wal-Mart. Or, God knows, inventory-less giant Dell Computer. It's been a distribution revolution. And FedEx has led the way ... been the Inventor-in-Chief.

We're not "at a crossroads." We're in the midst of a once-every-500-years-change. The very nature of commerce and community is being redefined. The compression of time ... the uncompromising demand for Top Quality ... Instantly ... Anywhere ... Everywhere ... is the universal plea ... and insistent demand.

> Is FedEx set for the future?
> Absolutely, positively not!

Many (including me) are in awe of FedEx ... and the revolution it has wrought. But FedEx knows (far better than I) that the Revolution (and don't forget to capitalize the R!) is only beginning. The Logistics-Time-Internet-Commerce-Life Revolution is still in diapers. It's been a heck of a 25 years ... and ... you/me ain't seen nothin' yet!!

Tom Peters wrote or cowrote *In Search of Excellence, A Passion for Excellence, Thriving on Chaos* and *Liberation Management*, all best-sellers in the U.S., Asia, Latin America and Europe. His most recent is *The Circle of Innovation: You Can't Shrink Your Way to Greatness*.

Courier Wong Xiau Yi
China

BY 1984, A YEAR WHEN FEDEX delivered 67 million packages and documents, the company was the undisputed leader in the express transportation industry. But there remained one unconquered territory: the international market. The company's entry into Canada during the late 1970s had enlarged the network and attracted new customers. But building a comprehensive international presence demanded determination, great expense and the courage to butt heads with already-established competitors. To North Americans FedEx may have been a household name, but few people overseas had ever heard of it.

The company's European presence began in 1984, when Federal Express bought the courier service Gelco Express International. The following year, the company chose Brussels, Belgium, as its European hub (later moved to Paris), and transatlantic two-day service premiered that summer. FedEx launched the service in a gala commercial featuring all of the overworked and speed-pressured characters who had ever appeared in the company's TV ads.

As the European business increased, FedEx looked to other regions of the world. Direct service to Mexico and Japan began in 1988. By the end of the decade, FedEx was providing delivery to more than 100 nations. Yet the international business was not a moneymaker, and landing rights remained difficult to come by in many countries. A new global strategy was needed.

For years, Federal Express and The Flying Tiger Line Inc., had flown in some of the same skies and frequently crossed paths. Flying Tigers, based in Los Angeles, was the world's largest cargo airline, with particularly strong links to Asia, Latin America and Europe.

In December 1988, FedEx announced its purchase of Flying Tigers for $880 million. Many industry analysts declared that Federal Express had at last reached too far, paying a high price for

Asia has been home to numerous FedEx innovations. The arrival of the first FedEx flight into Japan in 1988, shown here, was followed by next-business-day service between major markets.

a company whose recent performance had been less than stellar. But Flying Tigers possessed a big cargo fleet, unique and extensive operating authorities, and deep penetration in many markets. FedEx shined at carrying express freight. As one organization, they could achieve a great deal.

The combination of Flying Tigers' international route authorities, cargo fleet and strategically located airport facilities quickened the growth of the FedEx global distribution network. "Without this acquisition, FedEx today would still be a strong international player," says Mike Murkowski, now vice-president of marketing for FedEx's Latin American business, "but it would have been far more expensive to expand, and the pace of growth would have been slower."

Rather than simply giving Tigers employees new FedEx badges, FedEx offered welcoming parties and a reassuring orientation package. The company even paid for a yearbook Tigers employees produced about their old company. "We sent people out from FedEx to where the Tiger people were," says Vicki Cloud, who then worked in Personnel. "We were ambassadors of our company. It wasn't a top-level group of people — we sent couriers and customer service agents to say, 'Here's someone just like you.'"

Tigers employees responded. "Naturally there was concern at first, but we were also intrigued," explains Murkowski, who had worked at Tigers. "FedEx was seen as the class act in the industry, and it had a reputation for good employee relations. By the end, most people at Tigers were amazed by the humanity we saw at FedEx."

Just as valuable as Flying Tigers' people, equipment and experience were the landing rights it gave FedEx across the globe. These enabled FedEx to leapfrog to a powerful international position. FedEx gained traffic rights in such key markets as Hong Kong, Singapore, Malaysia, Seoul, Australia, Brazil and Venezuela. In Japan, where FedEx previously had government permission for just one daily flight in and out of the country, the Flying Tigers acquisition granted the

Moscow, Russia

79

company slots for six planes in Tokyo and the right to carry freight between the United States and Japan and other Asian destinations.

By 1997, the express-freight and traditional air-freight segment was moving over 600 million pounds of goods per year, representing more than half of FedEx's total international tonnage (the remainder were express documents and packages) and a significant part of international revenue.

CHAMPION OF OPEN SKIES The Flying Tigers acquisition energized FedEx international operations, but characteristic FedEx assertiveness helped just as much. No longer was it enough to be good at carrying express freight to other countries. To be successful, an international carrier continually had to secure and maintain international route authorities. Without the rights to land and use facilities across the globe, FedEx could not fly. Working closely with the U.S. Department of State and U.S. Department of Transportation, the company broke through many trade barriers. In 1990, FedEx pioneered the expansion of air-express services to Russia and the former Communist-bloc nations of Eastern Europe. In Taiwan, FedEx patiently negotiated for six years to gain its own cargo facilities. The company emerged as the only express carrier with the right to move intra-Asia traffic to and from Hong Kong, which has some of the world's most restrictive

THE CALL FROM A BIG MEDICAL LABORATORY IN PHOENIX was urgent. Shipments of amniotic fluid from two high-risk pregnancies had failed to arrive for testing. If they didn't come soon, the mothers-to-be would have to endure the difficult procedure again. • Senior customer service representative Brenda Currey got on the phone and found the shipments on a truck near Dallas. With help from FedEx operations staff, she had the truck stopped and 20,000 pounds of freight unloaded to retrieve the two samples. "Get them to Phoenix and I'll take care of them," Currey told the Dallas ramp manager. She met the flight carrying the shipments at 11 p.m., stored them in her refrigerator as instructed by the lab, and delivered them personally the next day. "Why did you do this?" asked a laboratory technician. "It needed to be done," Currey replied, "and I was there." • Three days later, the laboratory called to let Currey know that her efforts had paid off: The samples were just fine. • BRENDA CURREY, WITH FEDEX SINCE 1985

Istanbul, Turkey

When Flying Tigers joined FedEx, so did a menagerie of animals. Flying Tigers was expert at hauling not only big fish but also pandas, koala bears, thoroughbred horses and domestic livestock. In 1994, the Peregrine Fund asked FedEx to transport 12 of the world's 76 remaining California condors for relocation.

82

MADRID
ISTANBUL

air regulations. And in Latin America, FedEx has won access to more restricted points than any of its competitors.

Successes such as these enabled the international division to ring up its first profitable year in 1993. Soon FedEx — focusing its international business on service between North America and overseas — was giving customers access within 24 to 48 hours to a global network that topped 210 countries, representing 90 percent of the world's economic activity. Gradually, more of the world's nations were adopting "open skies" deregulation of trade, and FedEx could take pride in spearheading the effort to open those markets.

Back in the U.S., FedEx had another challenge to overcome. Forty-two states had attempted to regulate trucking operations, setting rates and restricting other aspects of service. FedEx believed it should be exempt from state regulations because its ground fleet was merely an extension of its network of interstate and international air links. So, 17 years after successfully lobbying against government airline regulation, FedEx was back in Washington to fight for comprehensive deregulation of the trucking industry. Its persistence paid off when Congress passed the legislation in 1994.

The deregulation had far-reaching effects. "Consumers were paying for this additional regulation," remembers Kenneth R. Masterson, now executive vice-president, general counsel and secretary of FDX Corporation. "If you were in Texas, it was cheaper to ship a pair of jeans from the Far East than from within Texas. Deregulation was estimated to bring in billions of dollars in

Goa, India

annual savings to U.S. consumers." Robert Delaney of Cass Information Systems agrees that FedEx's push for trucking deregulation improved the U.S. business climate: "Before that, every manufacturer had to operate its own private trucking fleet or use the alternative — commercial services that delivered terrible service and high costs."

By the mid-1990s, commerce of a different sort was gaining momentum. On the Internet, people could buy merchandise, read online magazines and communicate with one another instantly. Why not let customers use the Internet to order FedEx services and check on the status of their FedEx shipments? FedEx inaugurated its comprehensive World Wide Web site at www.fedex.com in 1994. Fred Smith observed: "We were originally formed as a child of the computer age to transport electronics and computer parts. Now we've become its progeny."

At the 25-year mark, the people of FedEx could look back proudly at a long list of accomplishments: $12 billion in annual revenues, more than 3 million packages handled every day, a fleet that made FedEx the fifth-largest airline in the world, and leadership of an express distribution industry that is $35 billion strong and growing yearly.

Just as FedEx made a creative leap a quarter century ago by discovering a new way to marry aviation with the delivery of goods, the company will use equal drive and imagination to carry its vision of service into the next 25 years and beyond.

Even if you subtract the outgoing Elvis Presley memorabilia, Memphis International Airport is still the world's largest cargo airport, with more than 2.2 million metric tonnes of cargo handled in 1997 alone.

85

IT WAS A HARRIED DAY IN AUGUST 1997 when an American plastic surgeon called the FedEx Pearl River, New York, office in desperation. The surgeon, who heads a nonprofit charity called Share, needed the cancer-fighting drug Cytoxin to help Kenyan children under her care. "I knew we had to do something," says Maureen Boylan, a senior invoicing specialist in Pearl River, near Share headquarters. • She appointed herself to go to Share's offices, where she picked up the six packages and completed the extensive paperwork required by the Kenyan government. Before heading out, she had gotten approval for FedEx to donate the shipment. "If a customer calls," she says, "you have to be able to help." Coworker Wendy Perry contacted managers, Boylan says, and "they all said go for it." • When Boylan discovered that civil unrest had caused the FedEx Kenyan affiliate to close temporarily, she made more calls. "We were able to notify them that the shipment was there, and they made the delivery." • MAUREEN BOYLAN, WITH FEDEX SINCE 1990

THE PRIDE OF FEDEX

BY DAVID PRYOR

It gives me great personal pleasure to be among those who are sending their congratulations on the occasion of Federal Express's 25th anniversary. The name Federal Express has become synonymous with pride, quality and customer service on a global scale. These principles have been borne out in the many awards FedEx has received for these worthy attributes. The history of the company clearly demonstrates the incredible power that ideas, innovation and perseverance can have in the free enterprise system.

I still remember fondly the first time I met Fred Smith — a young, energetic and idealistic entrepreneur who wanted to risk his inheritance to start an airline for packages. I thought to myself — that bright young man is going to lose his shirt — what a shame! It's a good thing Fred Smith didn't listen to me. Instead, he went out and through sheer determination and perseverance built a $12 billion global company serving hundreds of thousands of customers every day and literally changing the way the world works. Now, who can imagine doing business today without FedEx?

I have often thought — what is FedEx's secret weapon? I think I know. It's the EMPLOYEES. What a great group of dedicated and proud individuals. I observe your friendly faces and purposeful strides everywhere I go. FedEx is truly one of the best "people companies" in the world.

Federal Express has helped to make our world smaller, bring families and people throughout the globe closer together and changed the way people everywhere "do business" and communicate.

I salute the employees of Federal Express past and present, and wish you all the success in the future. I always enjoy asking couriers and other employees of Federal Express to tell me about their company. What pride they express in being associates in this great organization. They have every right to be proud to work for such a progressive company and exemplary corporate citizen. You have my great respect and admiration.

SINCE RETIRING FROM THE U.S. SENATE IN 1996, DAVID PRYOR HAS BECOME A FULBRIGHT DISTINGUISHED FELLOW OF LAW AND PUBLIC AFFAIRS AT THE UNIVERSITY OF ARKANSAS IN FAYETTEVILLE.

Memphis and FedEx: The Old and the New

By Richard Tillinghast

When Jud Williford, whose family has lived in Memphis for generations, treated his FedEx employees to lunch recently at the Little Tea Shop near the Mississippi River in downtown Memphis, the Old South ambience took them by surprise. Williford is manager of a group responsible for computer application architectures — system structures that control work flow at the shipping giant. Since most of them knew only the "new" Memphis, they were surprised by the slowed-down atmosphere of the Tea Shop, a traditional Memphis favorite. The fried okra, summer squash and turnip greens cooked with ham hocks seemed more typical of a small Southern town than of the fast-paced business city Memphis has become in the FedEx era.

Discussing Java development and ISDN connections while eating black-eyed peas and cornbread is typical of how this company and this city get along. FedEx, having brought 28,000 jobs to Memphis and made its airport the busiest in the world between midnight and 4 a.m., has profoundly affected this old river city and has, in turn, absorbed some of Memphis' ways.

While it might be an overstatement to say that FedEx has dragged the city kicking and screaming into the 1990s, it is no longer possible for Memphians to worry, as they once did, that progress has left them behind. In addition to its own presence in 60 different locations in the city, FedEx's delivery capabilities have drawn other industries here. The employees FedEx has attracted to this city from other parts of the country have brought their own accents and their own speeded-up sense of time with them.

But Memphis has put its stamp on FedEx as well. From its very beginnings, FedEx has encouraged individual initiative and innovative ways of doing business — a legacy, perhaps, of Memphis' early days as a frontier town in what, in the mid-19th century, was still regarded as the Southwest. I can think of no more perfect marriage of the old and the new than the way FedEx ships ribs and chopped pork shoulder from prime Memphis barbecue purveyors Corky's and the Rendezvous all over the country from the Memphis airport.

Historically, it makes sense that Memphis should be the home of a major transportation company. The city got its start as a port on the Mississippi River. Situated at the point where Tennessee meets the states of Mississippi to the south and Arkansas to the west, Memphis has traditionally been a marketplace for cotton from the Mississippi River Delta and lumber from surrounding forests. Walking around the neighborhood between Main Street and the river, you see all around you the old brick warehouses and cotton offices that once supplied this trade.

On a quiet morning in Memphis you can still hear foghorns from barges plying the Mississippi River. On a muggy summer night, the passage of a freight train brings back a sense of the city's mythical past, calling to mind the words of a hundred blues songs. But as the 21st century begins, the new sounds of commerce in Memphis come from FedEx jets taking off from the airport, 143 flights a night.

RICHARD TILLINGHAST, A NATIVE OF MEMPHIS, REVIEWS BOOKS AND WRITES ON TRAVEL FOR *THE NEW YORK TIMES* AND *THE WALL STREET JOURNAL*.

GLOBAL VISION

ON SEPTEMBER 2, 1997, a DC-10 loaded with time-sensitive cargo left a runway at Roissy

Charles de Gaulle Airport in Paris, headed for Dubai in the United Arab Emirates.

As transportation milestones go, this departure might not seem as momentous as the

completion of America's transcontinental railroad, the opening of Europe's

Chunnel, or humankind's *Apollo 11* journey to the Moon.

But for people who live and work on the brink of the 21st century,

the flight carried an economic and historic significance that only time

may fully make clear.

That's because this takeoff was the second leg of an inaugural

"around-the-world" flight by FedEx. The five-days-a-week flight, which

originates in America's heartland — Indianapolis, Indiana — makes possible

speeded-up distribution among markets that stretch from the United States to Europe, the

Middle East, India and Asia.

In 1973, FedEx invented an industry by launching a handful of aircraft to deliver goods

overnight among two dozen U.S. markets. Today, FedEx operates the world's most

extensive and integrated air and ground express distribution network. A net-

work capable of delivering packages and freight of virtually any

type, size or weight to markets that comprise 90 percent of the

world's total gross domestic product (GDP) — all within 24 to

48 hours. Door-to-door. Customs-cleared. With the industry's

highest standards of reliability.

"Today, companies must move fast, or they won't be moving at all."

MICHAEL HAMMER AND JAMES CHAMPY, *REENGINEERING THE CORPORATION*

When Temic Semiconductor decided to automate ordering, consolidate inventory and cut distribution time, it went for a total solution with FedEx.

Now, customers get electronic order confirmation in seconds and, at the same time, production is automatically scheduled at a Temic factory.

Inside the FedEx Subic Bay hub, FedEx employees pick, pack and ship Temic orders worldwide from an optimum level of inventory.

In the past, using conventional carriers, it took a week to 17 days for shipments to reach customers. Today, they reach Asia in less than 24 hours, North America within 48 hours and Europe within 72 hours.

Consolidating inventory at a single FedEx facility helped Temic close three warehouses, saving more than $5 million. Ongoing, rapid delivery from one site helps Temic trim inventory-related costs by more than $2.2 million annually.

Just how fast and far-reaching is FedEx? Consider that a cargo jet traveling at optimal speed, 550 miles per hour, needs more than 45 hours to circle Earth at its midsection. Essentially within that same time, FedEx spans oceans and continents, connecting merchants with customers, and manufacturers with suppliers, often as early as 8 a.m. each business day.

Of course, this feat involves more than merely travel. The 48-hour service window includes the time, technology and people needed to pick up a shipment, bring it to a regional sort station, rush it to the airport, fly it to a FedEx hub, sort it, fly it to a destination airport, clear it through customs, transport it to a FedEx station, load it into a courier van and deliver it to the recipient.

What's required to build a network that, on its 25th anniversary, links more than 210 countries, employs upward of 140,000 people and delivers more than 3 million shipments each business day? Vision. A clear picture of a world where trade barriers are continually challenged and cleared. A world where businesses source raw materials and parts globally, then move high-value goods quickly among continents and across time zones. A world where global information and transportation networks can, in fact, squeeze time and distance, creating competitive advantage for those who manage them best.

A quarter century into its existence, the FedEx network continues to move outward and forward. Fifty or 100 years from now, historians may fully assess the impact made by FedEx people, technologies and services on the way the world works.

But even at this early stage, one thing seems clear. As with every transportation advance throughout history, the most telling aspect of FedEx is not the network itself. It's the connectivity, the potential — the new horizons — that FedEx creates for those who use it.

EVERYWHERE

FedEx Box
Federal Express

Large

▶▶▶ Pull to open   Pull to open ◀◀◀

Designed for two 8½" x 11"
document stacks or small items.

☐ FedEx Priority Overnight®   ☐ FedEx Standard Overnight®   ☐ FedEx 2Day™   ☐ NEW FedEx First Overnight™   ☐ FedEx International Services   ☐ Saturday Delivery

FedEx
Federal Express®

THE INTERNATIONAL IMPERATIVE When a small or fledgling business looks across an ocean to search for opportunities, what it often sees first are challenges. Concerns about government instability, political unrest and regulation. Worries about finding skilled labor and modern infrastructure in developing nations.

Despite perceived obstacles, the *1997 FedEx Survey of Small Business Exporters* found that 75 percent of them planned to expand exporting in the near term. Bill Fraine, FedEx senior vice-president of worldwide sales, explains their attitude this way: "Globalization is what everyone is afraid of, and yet it is where everyone wants and needs to be. That is why exporters are increasingly relying on business allies with global expertise to help them gain access to new markets."

A global express-distribution network eliminates, or at least minimizes, real and imagined roadblocks to trade. It lets a company start selling in distant markets without the time, cost and decisions involved in establishing distributorships and regional warehouses in other countries. It helps exporters and importers clear regulatory and cultural hurdles by tapping into a ready-made distribution pipeline. It gives logistics specialists and traffic managers fast, predictable shipping services via a network that — in relative terms — is no more difficult to use than a long-distance phone line.

Micron Technology, Inc., knows the power of express distribution. During the 1980s and 1990s, the Boise, Idaho-based maker of semiconductor memory products saw several U.S. competitors leave the DRAM business as it battled to survive in this global, price-driven industry. Micron eventually emerged as one of the world's leading producers of dynamic random access memory, or DRAM.

In the past, Micron has relied primarily on forwarders to collect orders from Asian suppliers, consolidate Micron's freight with that of other shippers, and eventually secure space in planes bound for the United States. Occasionally, shipments arrived weeks after original order pickup.

Meanwhile, competitors in Asia found an edge, controlling costs and cutting prices by using just-in-time delivery to reduce raw-material investment.

"The traditional approach to international transportation forced us to hold inventory, and that meant holding extra costs," says Allan Edwards, logistics manager for Micron. "Because we couldn't risk a line-down situation, we could never get to that lowest possible level of just-in-time inventory, or enjoy its benefits."

Looking for a competitive equalizer, Micron turned to FedEx. With FedEx, partners all along the supply chain — conducting the series of material and information exchanges that occur between a business, its suppliers, its distributors and, finally, its customers — can plan based on a precise schedule.

Then there is the question of reliability. Because each supply-chain link must synchronize with the next to work effectively, dependable delivery is crucial.

Edwards recalls one instance when a shipment from Asia had missed its connection at the FedEx hub in Anchorage, Alaska. FedEx employees took it upon themselves to charter a small jet,

Purple paint is heavier, hotter and more difficult to apply than white paint. By limiting the amount of purple when it redesigned its logo and global identity, FedEx saved about $1,000 on one 53-foot-long tractor trailer alone. Using white paint also reduced the surface temperatures of FedEx aircraft by 40° F, so less energy was needed to cool the planes.

97

CARRIE HOYT HAD ARRIVED HOME ONE WINTRY FRIDAY night in 1996 when the phone rang. A 53-foot-long tractor trailer carrying FedEx freight had jackknifed in heavy snow west of Lake Tahoe, Nevada, spilling packages on Interstate 80 and snarling traffic for miles. She lived nearby — could she check things out? • Hoyt, a ramp transport driver at the time and now a courier, didn't hesitate. Maneuvering the mountain roads in her four-wheel-drive vehicle, she found the truck split in two and snow obscuring the scene. After seeing that the spilled freight had been retrieved by the highway patrol, she went to protect what remained at the truck, purchasing tarps to cover exposed boxes and single-handedly moving freight away from the gaping hole in the truck. When a rescue truck arrived, Hoyt rallied a dozen people to transfer 2,225 packages to safety, finishing the job at about 3 a.m. • "It was a wild party," Hoyt says. "We moved 30,000 pounds of freight into the other trailer and sent it on to Colorado, its ultimate destination. Every package made it on time." • CARRIE HOYT, WITH FEDEX SINCE 1985

FedEx may move at the speed of light, but it can't do it in the dark. When the electricity failed during package sorting in Riyadh, Saudi Arabia, the FedEx team improvised: They started up the courier vans, lined them up outside the station and worked by headlights until the job was done.

98

load boxes into the plane's seats and deliver the shipment to Boise on time.

To optimize inventory and planning at all levels of a supply chain, express distribution offers real-time shipment information, day and night, accessible from anywhere. FedEx technology lets shippers and consignees place and process orders, track shipment status, confirm deliveries and more. All day long, Edwards gets advance shipping notices and shipment-status reports via an electronic data-interchange link created for Micron by FedEx.

Edwards says it's invaluable that his express-distribution provider acts globally but thinks locally, offering global expertise and relationships as an integral component of service. "FedEx employees are on the ground, they speak the language, they know the culture," he says. "If you're not there, it's impossible to understand all the details and subtleties. With FedEx, it's like having your own transportation agent in every market in the world, someone who understands and can look out for your needs."

GLOBAL CONNECTIVITY Companies are discovering that there is a world of difference between sporadic, unpredictable transportation and fast, *time-definite* delivery. Today regional offices dispatch field technicians, manufacturers retool production lines, surgeons schedule cases

IT WAS ONE OF THE MORE UNUSUAL SHIPMENTS FedEx has ever carried: Several thousand copies of the Koran on CD-ROM, destined for an important event on Spain's Mediterranean coast. The cargo weighed in on arrival in Paris at four tons — 20 times heavier than the shipper had reported. These high-tech texts, cumulatively worth several thousand dollars, were to be gifts from the Saudi Arabian king and his ambassador to Spain. They had to arrive on time. But the Fokker 27 aircraft linking Paris and Madrid was not geared up for the overload. • For the Operations team in Spain, the answer was clear: Find an extra plane. Working in close cooperation with FedEx in France, the team secured a spare Boeing 727 and extra containers. Next, they spent three hours negotiating with Spanish authorities to let the 727 land in Madrid, then lined up hub services and additional crews. Their ingenuity paid off, and the CD-ROMs reached the resort town of Marbella at 5 p.m., ahead of the guests.

Hong Kong

FedEx planes make an average of 24 intercontinental flights per day, including six flights between the U.S. and South America, seven flights between the U.S. and Europe, and 11 flights between the U.S. and Asia.

100

and executives plan meetings based on the anticipated arrival of a FedEx package on a specific date, by a certain time.

By delivering on global service fundamentals each day, FedEx has helped a generation of companies expand beyond their home markets and prosper on a national and international scale. These customers also benefit from FedEx innovations they never see, such as the relentless pursuit of extensions to the FedEx worldwide network.

Nowhere is this expansion more evident than in Asia. In 1995, the company unveiled FedEx AsiaOne®, a regional express-distribution network patterned after the hub-and-spoke system FedEx developed in the United States in the early 1970s.

FedEx AsiaOne literally revolutionized the possibilities for logistics and distribution within Asia. For all its economic progress in recent decades, Asia's fragmented geography and vast expanses of ocean made it a challenging market in which to transport goods quickly and reliably. Before the FedEx AsiaOne network, in fact, late-in-the-day pickups and early-morning, next-business-day deliveries — advantages used and valued for years by shippers elsewhere — were virtually nonexistent in Asia.

FedEx AsiaOne effectively nudged the region's island and mainland nations closer. With a new FedEx hub at Subic Bay, the Philippines, the network allows next-business-day delivery by 10:30 a.m. between such major trade centers as Hong Kong, Singapore, Tokyo, Manila, Bangkok and Seoul.

FedEx also is enhancing connectivity between Asia and the rest of the world. In 1997, for example, FedEx added a first-ever nonstop, 12-hour daily flight from

Mexico City, Mexico

Osaka, Japan, to Memphis, Tennessee, to better connect Southeast Asia with trading partners worldwide. This lets companies in such places as Penang and Singapore enjoy a full day's production and still get next-business-day delivery (accounting for the international dateline) to markets throughout the United States and Canada as well as in Mexico City.

The unique flight also brought real meaning to the term "just-in-time" for Micron Technology. Factoring in the dateline, Micron's logistics manager Allan Edwards says, "FedEx's reliable, next-business-day delivery from Asia to Boise is an important operational advantage for our company."

FedEx continues to extend its presence in markets that are important to exporters and importers, increasing flight frequencies, forging electronic links with customs authorities for faster clearance, and negotiating for expanded route authorities.

FedEx aircraft routes — purchased, negotiated for, strategically expanded over the years — are the invisible infrastructure that makes possible the unique global access FedEx customers enjoy. For example, although other express carriers claim to offer shippers access to and within Asia, FedEx is the only one authorized to fly between Tokyo's Narita Airport and other points in Asia. As Michael Ducker, FedEx senior vice-president for the Asia Pacific region, says, "Not having a Tokyo 'spoke' in an Asian network is like not serving New York City in the United States."

Similarly, FedEx is the only U.S.-based, all-cargo carrier authorized to fly into major markets in China. And throughout Latin America and Europe, FedEx possesses a collection of routes that gives businesses enhanced access to more corners of the globe than any other carrier.

Courier Cathy Andrychuk
Vancouver, British Columbia, Canada

Prague, Czech Republic

STOCKHOLM

RIO DE JANEIRO

WORLD VIEW For businesses, the net effect of a networked economy is this: The time, costs and challenges involved in reaching distant markets are effectively gone. With an information and distribution infrastructure in place around the world, most business opportunities are just a day or two away, allowing even a small or start-up business to function globally from its own backyard.

A manifest from a FedEx flight to São Paulo, Brazil, hints at just how many industries are moving high-value goods internationally. Tractor parts, aircraft parts, electronics and prescription drugs from the United States. Watch components and electronic assemblies made in Japan. Fragrances from Switzerland. Auto parts inbound from Germany and Italy.

That same day, an outbound flight from Brazil to the United States and points beyond carried air compressors, medical devices, leather shoes, electronic devices, chemical compounds and dozens of other commodities.

Daily, more than $16 billion in goods and services changes hands worldwide — more than $6 trillion in global trade each year. Between 1950 and 1995, world trade grew at a pace nearly three times faster than the rate of growth in any of the world's industrialized nations.

PUERTO RICO

IT WAS AN ORDINARY SUNNY DAY, and Reynold Feliciano was making pickups and deliveries around southwestern Puerto Rico when his van failed to start. With time flying and some of his biggest customers still ahead, he searched for a solution that would get his shipments onto the 6:30 p.m. flight out of Mayaguez. "I remembered that I had a friend with a tow truck," Feliciano recalls. • With the FedEx van hitched up in back, Feliciano rode in the tow truck with his friend and continued his route. At each stop he opened the back of the disabled van to load and unload packages. He arrived at the airport on schedule. • Feliciano says he thought nothing of the extra effort — nor of the amusing sight he must have made. "I have always been involved with my customers," he says. "My utmost goal was to satisfy the customer on time, every time." • REYNOLD FELICIANO, WITH FEDEX SINCE 1982

The ability to access markets quickly and conveniently, no matter where one chooses to set up shop, lets a computer-chip maker operate a factory in a jungle in Singapore and lets a financial services company function from the plains of South Dakota, in the middle of the United States. Information links and express-distribution networks span borders and boundaries. Today global markets are not so much places on a map, as they are points on a global circuit. Connected. Accessible. Within slivers of time.

"Distance is disappearing as a limiting factor in all business operations," write consultants Stan Davis and Bill Davidson, authors of the book *2020 Vision*. "Thanks to sophisticated information and logistics linkages, businesses are relocating and reconfiguring their activities into global value-added chains, based on least cost and greatest expertise.… Global production systems, linked by global communications and logistics systems, are appearing in virtually all manufacturing industries and in a growing array of service businesses."

So whether a business is considering its first step into exporting or its next marketing thrust into an unexplored world market, the first question need not be, "How do we possibly begin?" but rather, "Where shall we do business today?"

WHAT HATH FEDEX WROUGHT?

BY AARON J. GELLMAN

 Federal Express represents the greatest discontinuity in transport history since the founding of commercial aviation itself. Indeed, FedEx and its early successes forced the world to reconsider several of the most fundamental assumptions underlying transportation economics.

FedEx demonstrated more dramatically than ever before that:

• Decisions regarding the movement of goods must consider total logistics costs, not just the transportation component of such costs;

• Line-haul transport costs for a wide variety of shipments often represent a relatively small part of total logistics costs; and that

• A hub-and-spoke route configuration, properly designed and managed, is well-suited to long-distance transportation of goods, even in the face of short transit times and great reliability.

What's more, the hub-and-spoke configuration FedEx pioneered enables both carriers and their customers to realize tremendous economies of scope: Carriers can serve a far broader set of points, and shippers can serve a greater range of markets, thus spurring their growth and often resulting in greater economies of scale in the production of their own products.

As FedEx grew in the mid-1970s at a pace and in ways the market clearly wanted, it was constrained by the economic regulation of air transportation in the United States, the company's only geographic market in the early years. Largely as a result of FedEx's efforts, the economic regulation dominoes began to fall in 1978; within two years deregulation had spread not only to air transportation but to surface transport as well. The continuing spread of economic deregulation today in a variety of industries — from transport to energy to banking and communications — owes much to FedEx's early campaign to free up air-freight transportation in the United States.

FedEx innovated on the operational level as well, benefiting not only itself and its customers but also its competitors and even other industries. Perhaps most significant was the way FedEx recognized the value and role of data and information in transport and logistics.

Certainly FedEx was the first enterprise in the world to understand the market power of providing real-time tracking and tracing ability as an integral component of a transportation "product." FedEx correctly perceived that its customers want to know where their shipments are with reliability and precision; FedEx responded as no one had before. But that is not all. The company found that such information allowed it to manage its own operations more precisely and help it spot threats to reliability (and even to efficiency) and deal with them in an aggressive, timely way.

The FedEx market and management success was not lost on others. Especially as economic deregulation swept the landscape, railroads, truckers, forwarders and shippers began to emulate FedEx as best they could. In this way FedEx pushed even its competitors, including postal services over much of the world, to become more efficient.

The hallmark of FedEx service has always been reliability. FedEx illustrated just how highly the market prizes reliability by its own impressive results in every market it serves. And FedEx has shown that a high level of reliability is practically possible and sustainable even as the scale and scope of the enterprise doubles and redoubles. FedEx reliability continues to set new, higher standards for transport and logistics firms, a fact that has contributed materially to reductions in inventory-related costs.

The FedEx emphasis on reliability, speed of service and broad market coverage combined to enable customers of all sizes to reach far more markets than ever before, and to do so without significant increases in inventory and attendant costs. Thus, it became clear that shippers could profitably use the "premium" express services offered by FedEx on a routine basis because the benefits substantially outweighed the costs.

Throughout its quarter-century history, FedEx has continued to set the standards for logistics and transport services by which all others are judged. This reflects leadership of a high order that promises continued innovation for many years to come.

AARON J. GELLMAN, PH.D., IS DIRECTOR OF THE TRANSPORTATION CENTER AT NORTHWESTERN UNIVERSITY IN EVANSTON, ILLINOIS, AND PROFESSOR AT ITS KELLOGG GRADUATE SCHOOL OF MANAGEMENT AND ITS MCCORMICK SCHOOL OF ENGINEERING AND APPLIED SCIENCE.

IN THE FUTURE, moving products and information in fast, time-certain fashion will not simply be one approach to doing business — it will be *the* way business is transacted.

Global trade is on a fast track. Since the 1950s, the value of intercontinental cargo transported by air has grown faster than total world gross domestic product. Research by the aeronautics giant Boeing suggests that the express share of worldwide cargo shipments will swell from 5 percent in 1995 to nearly 40 percent by 2015.

What's the rush? Businesses recognize, as never before, the value of streamlining logistics — the storage, time and cost involved in converting raw materials into finished goods, then delivering them to customers.

Traditionally, manufacturers of high-value products — computers, software, pharmaceuticals, medical devices, auto parts, optics, avionics, high-fashion apparel — invested heavily in inventory to fill regional distribution centers and dealer warehouses. These same businesses generally sought the least-expensive method for transporting finished goods to customers.

But assets that sit idle exert drag on a balance sheet. And if too much inventory languishes inside a warehouse, a sudden shift in consumer taste or a major innovation by a competitor can render entire batches obsolete.

Now add the labor, insurance and fixed costs of maintaining regional distribution facilities, and it becomes clear why a garment maker, a cellular-phone manufacturer or a digital TV distributor would turn to express distribution to shorten the cycle time from when a product is ordered to when it is delivered.

In John Wallace's business, time is critical. As chief operating officer of Nova Biomedical

"As a strategic weapon, time is the equivalent of money, productivity, quality, even innovation."

George Stalk Jr.

Corporation, a maker of blood-diagnostic devices based in Waltham, Massachusetts, Wallace and his colleagues know that a malfunctioning machine or a single back-ordered part might have serious consequences for a hospital and its patients.

With global competitors poised to snatch away dissatisfied customers, Nova has committed to a "zero-back-orders" service standard. When a customer calls to order a new diagnostic device, a part or reagent fluids, that order must be processed and shipped the same day and then delivered within a one- or two-business-day deadline. No questions. No excuses.

Prior to Nova making its no-back-order pledge, roughly 85 percent of its orders (250 per day, on average) reached customers on time. Today, the standard is 100 percent, owing to Nova's stringent internal processes and to FedEx. Over more than two and a half years, Nova customers experienced just one back order — a product that arrived at its destination less than 24 hours late — and that one was the result of paperwork being temporarily misplaced. In a recent survey, Nova customers rated order delivery their No. 1 point of satisfaction.

Turning inventory a minimum of 10 times each year is another way Nova competes in time. Because health care is increasingly competitive, hospitals are seeking cost efficiencies, including the costs of diagnostic supplies and parts. Pressured to deliver products on a fast-response basis, Nova has two options: Either assume the inventory costs customers are unwilling to absorb — by stockpiling parts and supplies at distribution sites — or keep the barest levels of inventory at a central location and rely on express distribution to fill orders.

Not surprisingly, Nova chooses the latter. "Inventory is always on the balance sheet as an asset, but I consider it a liability," Wallace says. "We should have enough but not too much."

FedEx flies the longest daily nonstop cargo flight in the world, between Osaka, Japan, and Memphis, Tennessee. The 12-hour, 7,000-mile flight is so long that the four MD-11 aircraft assigned to the route were outfitted with special sleeping compartments for off-duty crew members.

Since working with FedEx, Nova has grown from a company that generates $45 million in revenue on inventory of $17 million to an $80 million enterprise on inventory of just $6 million.

A shrewd manager might question whether premium costs for express distribution erode Nova's inventory savings. Wallace says quite the opposite. "When we look at cost, we look at 'total' cost," he says. "Total cost is everything, not just the cost of service, but how easy FedEx is to work with, their professionalism, their agility, their online systems, the satisfaction of our customers. When you look at those costs compared with everyone else, I'd say FedEx is a bargain."

BUYING TIME As the Nova Biomedical example shows, today's end users exert their own forms of time pressure on businesses. Given access to a "global bazaar" of goods and services, customers are basing purchase decisions on a cumulative set of demanding standards.

At one point in the 20th century, cost was the primary issue. In response, businesses across any number of industries moved aggressively to streamline and automate, squeezing margins to get in line with the competition.

In the 1970s and 1980s, product and service quality issues took center stage, forcing Western businesses to play catch-up by implementing continuous improvement lessons such as those taught to the Japanese by esteemed management consultants W. Edwards Deming and Joseph Juran.

In any given product category, technology can be the primary point of distinction. But where once a patent might have bought a company decades of breathing room, competition from all parts of the world now tends to make breakthroughs in many industries frequent, incremental and short-lived.

Now *time* has emerged as a largely untapped source of advantage. Product features, quality

Rafael Cedeno at Nova Biomedical scans parts before packing them for shipment.

and price being equal, most customers prefer to have their orders filled, systems configured, equipment repaired and transactions processed sooner rather than later.

Faced with customers who are in a hurry, businesses must compete not only on all the earlier standards — cost, quality and technological innovation — but also on time, with time increasingly becoming the key factor separating market leaders from followers and failures. Tracy Schmidt, chief financial officer and senior vice-president, finance, at FedEx, says: "Frankly, it's now to the point where customers have to compete in time as simply an ante into the game. It's no longer a luxury. It's an essential element of business."

How are businesses responding? By moving — their production, thinking and shipping — faster. Although only 2 percent of worldwide cargo tonnage currently moves by air, that amount represents *40 percent* of the monetary value of global trade. Factor out agricultural products and petroleum, and suddenly half the value of goods traded globally is being ordered and delivered in fast-cycle mode.

Where businesses once used express distribution only as a "rush" or emergency solution, they're now wielding it as a competitive weapon. In the United States alone, the express share of cargo distribution is expected to surge from its 1994 level of 39 percent to 53 percent by 2002.

George Stalk Jr., of The Boston Consulting Group, who conducts extensive research on time-based competition, put it this way in the *Harvard Business Review*: "The best competitors, the most successful ones, know how to keep moving and always stay on the cutting edge. Today, *time* is on the cutting edge.

On its first day of service in Beijing, FedEx received 900 packages — about 450 more than it had anticipated. In a rush, the entire start-up team pitched in to sort and deliver, carrying packages through the city center in plastic laundry baskets. It was a clean sweep, with all packages delivered on time.

New Territories, Hong Kong

"We will see the rise of more and more companies —

such as Federal Express which epitomizes that newest

and rarest breed of company — that can fully synergize

technology and business to create a company that is the

essence of 'the competitive use of information technology.'"

JESSICA KEYES, *INFOTRENDS: THE COMPETITIVE USE OF INFORMATION*

"The ways leading companies manage time — in production, in new product development and introduction, in sales and distribution — represent the most powerful new sources of competitive advantage."

In the global economy it helped create, FedEx continues to move full speed ahead. In January 1992 alone, the company opened service to 23 African countries: 235 million people spread over 13.1 million square kilometers. In 1995, eight countries of the former Soviet Union gained service in a single month.

116

LEVERAGE FROM LOGISTICS By textbook definition, logistics is the process of planning, implementing and controlling the efficient, effective flow and storage of goods, services and related information from the point of origin to the point of consumption.

Businesses are discovering that logistics — previously treated by many as a cost-driven, back-office afterthought — presents opportunities to innovate. Many experts, in fact, see it as one of the few remaining areas where a company can cut costs while improving customer service.

How? By removing time and cost from the process, in order to reinvest those precious resources in research and development, product customization and quick-response distribution.

Stalk and Thomas M. Hout, authors of *Competing Against Time: How Time-Based Competition Is Reshaping Global Markets*, found that time-savvy companies generally are able — at a minimum — to grow three times faster than competitors and achieve profits more than twice their industry averages.

Louis Vuitton leather goods and products enjoy a worldwide reputation for quality. The company's brand excellence is enhanced by an express-distribution solution developed with FedEx.

More than 60 U.S. stores place weekly orders to a central, fully automated distribution facility near Paris. There a FedEx shipping-automation system streamlines shipment processing.

"Time-based competitors are offering greater varieties of products and services, at lower costs and in less time than are their more pedestrian competitors," the authors note. "In so doing, they are literally running circles around their slower competition."

In other words, reducing logistics cycle time actually creates more time — a different kind of time. Time to be creative. Time to customize. Time to innovate and add value for customers.

National Semiconductor knows the power and profitability of time. In the early 1990s, the Sunnyvale, California, company — one of the world's largest semiconductor makers — embarked on an initiative to rethink its global logistics, squeezing out time and cost at every step along the way.

In an industry in which 10 months is the typical product life cycle and even a few days' reduction in inventory costs can trigger millions in savings, National recognized that a seven- to 21-day distribution cycle meant its profitability and competitive position were vulnerable.

Closer analysis revealed that 14 days was typical to move an order from the factory to the customer. What's more, National was using no fewer than 42 forwarders and 14 airlines to ship orders worldwide.

When it decided to seek help from a logistics expert, National selected FedEx. In the end, National turned over its entire logistics operation to FedEx and allowed FedEx to integrate the

● BANGKOK

● NEWPORT

117

A special FedEx service lets shipments to multiple stores clear U.S. customs as a single unit. Stores receive their orders within 10 days, compared with more than 30 days when the company used traditional freight forwarding.

By eliminating supply-chain inefficiencies, such as regional warehouses and customs delays, FedEx enables Louis Vuitton stores to order more precisely, trim inventory and respond quickly to customers' needs.

Musa Abdullah collects chips for fast-cycle distribution from National Semiconductor's Singapore facility.

organizations' information systems. As a result, National now enjoys global visibility of its inventory, both the products stored briefly at a FedEx warehouse in Singapore and those speeding to market inside "mobile warehouses" — FedEx planes, trucks and courier vans.

National's delivery cycle now averages two business days to any point in the world. The company closed or downsized nine distribution centers and reduced its logistics staff by 500, reassigning employees to focus on core business activities.

Kelvin Phillips, National's director of worldwide logistics, says having FedEx manage logistics made the difference between fine-tuning a broken process and creating a better way to do business. "We spent a lot of time discussing how we could trim a little here, get a 10-percent gain there," says Phillips, "but what we really needed was a radical redesign of our entire logistics."

During a period in which National's sales doubled, FedEx services helped the company trim $8 million in logistics costs, reducing logistics as a portion of overall operating costs from 3 percent to under 2 percent.

National Semiconductor is a dramatic example of what two organizations can accomplish when each focuses on its core competency — the business practices and processes it knows and does best. Other examples have followed.

When Insight, a direct marketer of computers, hardware and software, found itself challenged by shipping delays and other distribution inefficiencies, the company asked FedEx for a solution. FedEx consultants worked with a team from Insight to design a cleaner, more reliable pipeline to the marketplace. Today, 90 percent of in-stock orders ship via FedEx by 5 p.m. the same day. Having FedEx personnel on-site at Insight's distribution center

JAKARTA

CARTAGENA

119

Courier Diane Gotelli
San Francisco, California

Around the world in 80 days? FedEx goes that far five times a week! Every weekday morning at 3:10 a.m., a FedEx DC-10 flies east from Indianapolis, Indiana, then returns home from the west after stops in Paris, Dubai, Mumbai, Bangkok, Subic Bay in the Philippines and Anchorage, Alaska.

120

enables packages to be loaded into cargo containers and taken directly to the airport.

In another example, more than 20 businesses have opened primary distribution centers in Memphis, taking advantage of a unique "hub-based logistics" program in which FedEx helps them significantly reduce warehousing and inventory carrying costs by eliminating redundant regional distribution sites. FedEx does much of the advance planning and coordination required to help a company either lease or build a centralized warehouse. By operating virtually next door to the Memphis SuperHub, these businesses can leverage late cutoff times and use the full range of FedEx express and nonexpress services to improve service commitments and enhance product value to customers in the United States and throughout the world.

Of course, no two supply chains are identical. And no two products and customers are alike. That's why FedEx operates an entire division, called Logistics, Electronic Commerce and Catalog, that blends FedEx distribution and information-management assets to create tailored solutions for even the thorniest logistical challenges.

Overall, experts agree, a business that focuses on strategically managing its logistics can reduce its order-fulfillment cycle time, cut inventory carrying costs and position itself to deliver greater value and innovation to the marketplace faster.

And that's why, for most businesses, there's no time like the present to begin. After all, there are customers waiting.

Courier Luiz Monteiro
Rio de Janeiro, Brazil

PACKET SWITCHING

BY NICHOLAS NEGROPONTE

For me, the world is divided into two parts: atoms and bits. The difference between a piece of rock and a piece of information is that one has size, shape, color and mass, while the other does not. The consequence is huge. For example, bits are weightless so they can travel at the speed of light; they are formless so they don't take up any space; and the marginal cost of manufacturing more is zero.

These extraordinary properties will alter employment and commerce dramatically. Our great-grandchildren will be in the bit business — making them, finding them, distributing them, personalizing them and so on. Most atom businesses, such as manufacturing, will be driven by information about their products, versus the products themselves, just like banks are to bullion today.

In this new world of bits, many old and seemingly basic concepts will change. For example, how meaningful will the nation state be to commerce (bits don't stop at customs)? What will the balance of trade mean? Will there be any economic value in being big? But the biggest change will come from the phenomenon of disintermediation: the removal of unnecessary middlemen. For example, anybody with a job today that has the word "agent," "broker" or "wholesaler" in it, likely will find that job gone in 25 years or sooner.

Consider a bookstore. The reason to go to a bookstore is anything but buying a book. It is to browse, get advice, meet someone or to have some experience other than buying the book. In fact, if you know what book you want, you are best advised to buy it over the Internet. It will be cheaper and take you almost no time at all. This is obvious.

What is less obvious is that this can apply to all shopping. In fact, 25 years from now, the only reason for retail will be browsing. When you find something you want, you are likely to go home and buy it over the Internet. This not only applies to buying a Ford or a Swatch, but you'll be able to buy art directly from the artist, bread from the baker and wine from the vineyard. In other words, it is not only travel and real estate agents who will be disintermediated, but the entire retail chain will be turned upside-down.

I was asked not to write about Federal Express, but I cannot resist. If the above is only half true, I expect Memphis to turn into a giant warehouse where many manufacturers can keep an inventory of items for next-day delivery. This would apply equally to large appliance makers and grandmas making jelly. More generally speaking, the world of atoms has to learn from the world of bits. A last example — value-added atoms. Here's what I mean:

The telecommunications industry is studying how to add value to bits with services that, for example, help you navigate the digital world, maintain your privacy, or personalize and filter the tidal waves of information and entertainment. As a bit moves through the network, its value can be increased and you are billed for that change. This can be applied to atoms as well.

I use FedEx to send myself clean shirts on long trips and send the dirty ones home by the same means. Wouldn't it be nice if they were cleaned in Memphis? I am sure that 25 years from now, people will think of all sorts of ways to add value to atoms in a new age of packet switching.

PROFESSOR NICHOLAS NEGROPONTE IS DIRECTOR AND COFOUNDER OF THE MIT MEDIA LAB IN CAMBRIDGE, MASSACHUSETTS, AND AUTHOR OF *BEING DIGITAL*.

FOR EXPERIENCED SHIPPERS, picking up the phone or going on the Internet to check a shipment's status in real time, anywhere in the world, must by now seem almost mundane.

Yet it wasn't long ago that real-time shipping information was something corporate traffic managers only dreamed about. With traditional cargo service, people had little choice but to wait and wonder whether a shipment was getting to its destination as planned.

FedEx recognized early on that, for companies sending time-sensitive shipments to distant destinations, information about the shipment's status en route is nearly as important as the shipment itself. So, soon after FedEx introduced express distribution, it also revolutionized the precision with which logistics can be managed by giving customers real-time shipment information.

FedEx technologists continue to explore the leading edges of the industry, finding new and innovative ways to integrate information systems with global distribution. So much so, in fact, that *Wired* magazine has described FedEx as nothing less than "the Airline of the Internet."

After 25 years, the list of innovations and industry firsts streaming forth from FedEx testing labs runs long. In addition to a global shipment-tracking network called COSMOS® and hundreds of thousands of FedEx PowerShip shipping workstations for customers, there's also FedEx Ship software, capable of turning almost any customer's PC into a powerful shipping-management device. And FedEx interNetShip℠, which lets customers create shipping labels, request courier pickups, even send e-mail notification to recipients of the shipment, all from the fingertip convenience of the FedEx Web site. At last count, 750,000 FedEx customers were connected directly with FedEx to execute their shipping transactions fast and efficiently.

With its enterprise computers now handling more than 60 million information requests and

"Time is the scarcest resource and unless it is managed nothing else can be managed."

PETER F. DRUCKER

Courier Martin Filipek
Czech Republic

transactions each day, FedEx ranks not only as the world's largest express-distribution company but also as one of the world's busiest data-processing centers. By the year 2000, the total available capacity of the FedEx global network will be 16 billion bits per second across the wide-area network. In 1987, it was just 2.5 million bits.

FedEx continues to expand its "virtual" network — the logistics, electronic commerce and information-management solutions it makes available to customers — much as it continues to enlarge its physical network.

A prime example is FedEx FullView™, an order-fulfillment and inventory-visibility system that can help manufacturers, wholesalers and other suppliers ship parts and products directly to retail stores and other end customers. It is currently being developed so businesses can improve customer service while avoiding the cost and complexity of maintaining regional distribution centers.

Take a retailer in search of a special-order power tool or video game from a supplier. FedEx FullView will let parties on both ends of the transaction see inventory stock levels and order detail. Checking the system at 2 p.m. in Oakland, California, the retailer sees that he can order the product and commit to having it delivered by 10:30 a.m. the next business day, even though that product sits on a supplier's warehouse shelf more than 3,000 miles and three time zones away.

By enabling so-called vendor-direct ordering and distribution, FedEx FullView will create several advantages for the retailer — or for virtually any business that buys parts and products in volume. First, it can eliminate the fixed costs of operating multiple regional

For years, FedEx transported shipments in passenger aircraft reconfigured for freight. Now, FedEx is helping custom-design a plane from the ground up that's made for hauling freight. Called the Ayres LM-200 Loadmaster, the new aircraft emphasizes reliability, cost-efficient operation, flexibility and carrying capacity.

To speed up loading and unloading, the Loadmaster's wing will be high off the ground, the cargo door will be located toward the rear, and two engines will power a single, nose-mounted propeller.

The Loadmaster will support the rest of the FedEx fleet primarily on intermediate-length routes (200 to 400 miles), enabling FedEx to continue to enhance its service to small and medium-sized cities. The first of 50 new Loadmasters is scheduled for delivery in late 1999.

125

When high-value, high-risk ship-ments are transported around the world, FedEx is the carri-er of choice. From 1996 through 1998, FedEx worked with Iridium, Motorola's satellite communications division, to transport 72 satellites from the U.S. to launch sites in China and Russia. The satellites carry a new technology that permits any type of telephone transmission — voice, paging, fax or data — to reach its destination anywhere on Earth.

warehouses and inventory stockpiles, replacing them with a flexible, cost-effective alternative — express distribution from numerous vendor sites.

In addition, by using FedEx, the retailer improves customer service dramat-ically. Rather than guess when an inbound shipment might arrive, the salesperson can commit with confidence to a one-, two- or three-business-day delivery schedule, depending on which FedEx service he or she chooses.

Driving even deeper into the customer's operation, FedEx FullView™ will automate steps and reduce time and cost throughout order processing and fulfillment. For example, as a part or product is ordered, FedEx FullView will automatically generate a "pick ticket" and an address label at the supplier's warehouse. Once the shipment reaches the Oakland store, a quick scan of a bar code is enough to update inventory and set in motion the accounts payable process.

ONLINE OPPORTUNITY Besides making traditional sales and distribution systems dramati-cally more responsive and cost-effective, FedEx melds technology and logistics to help business establish new channels for growth. Case in point: the Internet.

According to Forrester Research, the total value of goods and services traded via the Internet will top $320 billion by 2002, compared with less than $10 billion in 1997. Despite projected "hypergrowth" in electronic commerce, many businesses are still searching for the key to unlock even modest returns from their Internet investments.

In response, FedEx was among the first express carriers to give customers entrée to the world of E-commerce. FedEx's consulting expertise and online publishing tool, FedEx VirtualOrder℠, make it possible for a business to launch — often within just a few days — an online product

FedEx interNetShip™
● Click here for contact information around the globe.

ALASKA

RIK PERRON AND WARD BLAIR BRAVE WHITEOUTS, DARKNESS, potholes and polar bears to
do their jobs. Each takes turns being the sole FedEx employee in Deadhorse, Alaska, north of the Arctic Circle, followed by a week back at the
FedEx office in Anchorage. • Sharing dormitory-like quarters in Deadhorse with an Alaska Airlines crew, they spend 10 to 11 hours a day scanning,
sorting, wrapping, loading and unloading up to 2,500 pounds of freight, handling paperwork, and driving a FedEx van over gravel roads and a
causeway to rigs drilling in the Arctic Ocean. Out there, says Perron, "there's nothing between you and the North Pole." • Perron and Blair volunteered for the route when FedEx opened it in 1991. The 2,000 to 3,000 workers in the Alaskan oil fields depend on FedEx for
everything from computer components to mechanical parts. "It feels like we're playing a big part in helping the operation
of the oil field," Blair says. • Reminded that windchills can plunge to 100° F below zero, Perron shrugs. "I can't think of
another route I'd rather have." • RIK PERRON (RIGHT), WITH FEDEX SINCE 1985; WARD BLAIR (LEFT), WITH FEDEX SINCE 1986

catalog and order-management system, creating a 24-hour-a-day channel to the global marketplace.

FedEx also develops electronic commerce solutions that help businesses easily integrate online order entry into their existing information systems. The result is a full-time, all-the-time "electronic sales force" that lets businesses focus more of their resources and people on building account relationships and exploring new, high-potential direct-sales markets.

According to the *1997 FedEx Survey of Small Business Exporters*, nearly 80 percent expect to use the Internet to conduct business before the year 2002. Thanks to worldwide connectivity, corporations are cropping up and starting strong based on little more than a unique marketing approach and a time-driven logistics strategy, plus the power and reach of express distribution.

This particular brand of Information Age venture doesn't even require an office building or warehouse, just so long as it resides firmly in the mind's eye of its founder. A visionary in the computer or personal electronics industry, for example, can generate orders via the Web, negotiate with a chain of suppliers to pull together components, outsource the assembly in Malaysia, and do it all on a made-to-order, fast-cycle basis, working from a garage in Montana. A kitchen-table capitalist in Chicago or an established manufacturer in Singapore can launch a Web site for their products and within 24 hours be taking orders from Turkmenistan and New Zealand.

FedEx's Laurie Tucker predicts it is the smaller and start-up companies — and those larger

CAIRO

TORONTO

"I think people have not recognized yet

what a powerful engine of change the Internet

will be. I think it is going to allow people to

sell and source things without regard to

time and place. That's never been true in

the history of the world."

FRED SMITH INTERVIEW, *FORBES® GREAT MINDS OF BUSINESS*

PERTH
PORTLAND

companies that act and think nimbly — that will find it easiest to adapt to the new business paradigms made possible by the networked economy. As senior vice-president of FedEx's Logistics, Electronic Commerce and Catalog division, Tucker devotes much of her time and energy to helping customers discover the precise blend of transportation, logistics and information management that will fuel new levels of profitability and productivity within their supply chains.

"Most large corporations are entrapped by departmental territorialism and hierarchy," Tucker says. "Only those led by aggressive, gutsy leadership will take on the daunting task of disaggregating past practices, eliminating mass from the enterprise and reengineering distribution.

"The small and mid-size companies are pliant," she adds. "And new companies may enter a market with a totally new approach, a virtual approach. By relying on best-of-class providers in the various facets of their business, virtual companies benefit from keeping overhead low and by leveraging the investment made by the experts."

Using FedEx VirtualOrder℠, for example, one computer hardware and parts distributor quickly developed an online "Webalog" to replace its traditional product catalog. The company realized considerable savings on printing, saw its sales climb 10 percent per month, and found the vast majority of its new customers dialing in from untapped global markets. When the time came, FedEx delivered the distributor's products to such far-off locations as Venezuela and the Ukraine. Getting the order. Delivering the goods. More and more, customers are finding FedEx a strategic ally on both ends of the business transaction.

Besides using technology to open new markets for customers, FedEx applies its information-systems expertise to help customers reach those markets with shipments that speed more quickly through global customs checkpoints.

For many businesses, customs regulations are the most daunting obstacles to exporting. That's why FedEx has worked hard to establish electronic data-interchange connections with customs authorities. By transmitting information about a shipment electronically to the destination country — typically while that shipment is in the air, hours from its destination — the FedEx ExpressClear^{SM} Electronic Customs Clearance system sets the stage for prompt clearance and on-time delivery for an ever-increasing percentage of the world's time-sensitive shipments.

Electronic sharing and processing of customs clearance information is available on more than 80 percent of the shipments moving through the FedEx network. Of the thousands of shipments that arrive at the FedEx Memphis, Anchorage and Paris hubs each business day, the vast majority clear customs that same day. That level of performance — the best in the express industry — means shippers are serving their global customers more reliably and deleting time and cost from their logistics processes.

James Wetherbe, author of *The World On Time,* a book that analyzes the foundational management principles of FedEx, observes that "FedEx has proved — more conclusively than most other companies — that the information an organization creates and shapes has value far beyond its in-house uses."

The FedEx Web site at www.fedex.com gives easy access to FedEx around the world. The site includes more than 3,000 pages of information, in six languages, with specialized information for 200-plus countries. It receives an estimated 5 million visits per month, and customers track the status of more than 2 million packages per month.

131

A WORLD ON THE MOVE For businesses and business managers of the future, old formulas will no longer apply. Economies of size will not necessarily ensure success. Corporate hierarchies and traditional approaches will no longer guarantee market leadership. Not when global

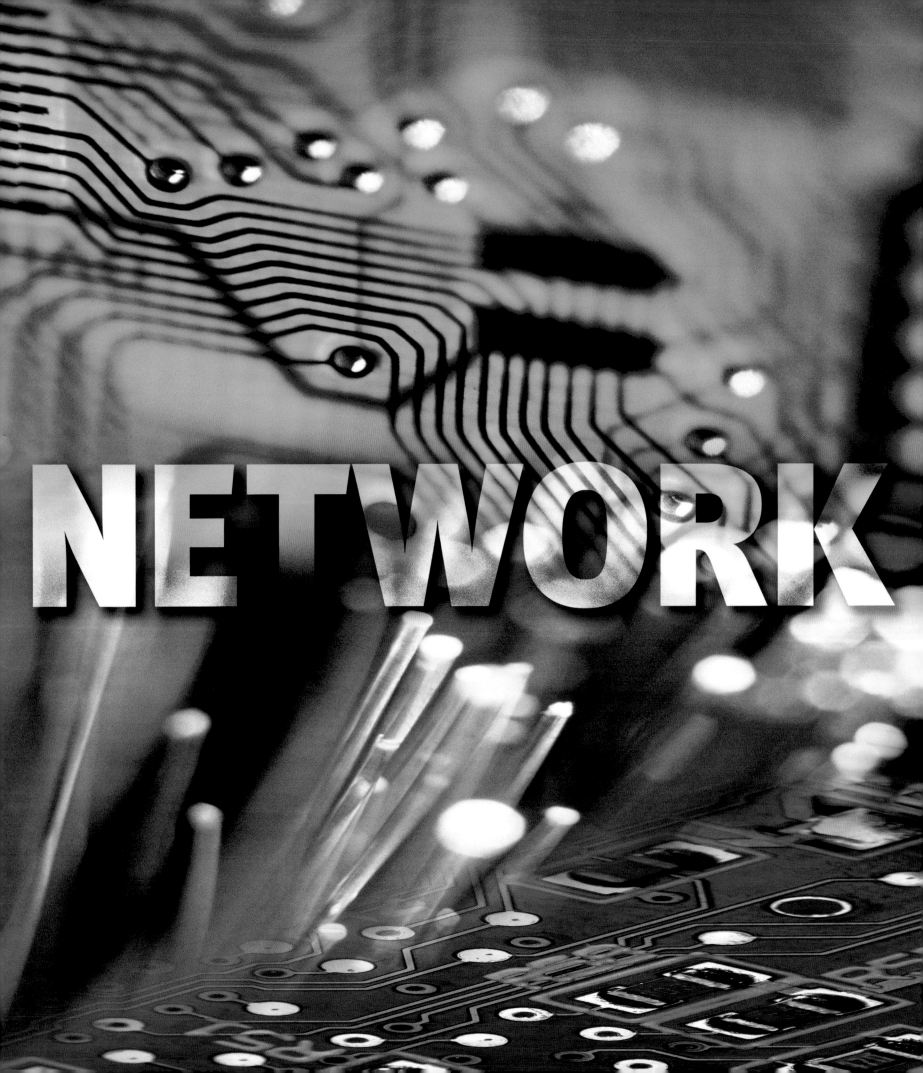

networks afford virtually every organization equal and near-instant access to a world of economic opportunities. Not when FedEx makes it possible for companies to aggressively get into the global economy, effectively get out of the inventory and transportation business, and move forward focused on the products, services and processes at which they truly excel.

Joseph McCarty, corporate vice-president and chief administrative officer of FDX, looks ahead to what he believes is a business landscape about to be transformed.

For example, before the year 2000, economic forecasts are calling for countries in Latin America to outpace their trade partners in Asia and assume the well-traveled title of "world's fastest-growing economic region." During that same period, McCarty predicts, people and businesses in regions around the world will begin to recognize the full power, the true potential, of a fast, globally interconnected economy.

"If you talked to someone in 1947 about the telephone in their home, no one at that point understood the phone's true power," McCarty says. "If you look at how some people and businesses view FedEx, they see us pretty much like that 1947 phone. Instead of seeing the power of the global connectivity, the power of the network to revolutionize how and where they do business, they simply see us as an instrument for sending something from here to there.

"But what this system, this network, really does is take away all the disadvantages. The disadvantages of geography. The disadvantages of size and lack of global experience and sophistication. We've essentially created an Internet for shipping and distribution. And when people in business really begin to think about that, really see that for the first time, I think they'll find their world opening up in remarkable new ways."

FedEx kept the Rolling Stones rolling during their 1995 Voodoo Lounge tour, which made 120 stops across six continents. FedEx moved all the production materials for the show, including 300 tons of fragile sound and lighting equipment.

133

THE NETWORKED ECONOMY

BY JIM BARKSDALE

I'm honored to be asked to participate in FedEx's 25th-anniversary book since I was a member of that team for half of its 25 years. I learned many great lessons there about the value of networks, both on the systems side as chief information officer and later as chief operating officer. Those lessons have stayed with me in my work with two other networking companies: McCaw Cellular, the world's largest cellular company, which is now part of AT&T; and Netscape, the Internet company.

Networks — whether they are physical distribution networks such as the one Federal Express has built or electronic networks such as the Internet and cellular phone networks — have the same underlying principles and values. A point-to-point network grows in value exponentially as the number of endpoints grows. This is because you never know how all the points of commerce are going to intersect. You can't size a bridge by counting the swimmers — a bridge creates traffic just as a network creates traffic. Every endpoint that's added can then be connected to all the other endpoints. That's what makes networks great economic engines. This was a lesson we all learned together as we expanded the FedEx network to circle the globe.

As we move into the next millennium, the value of networks will become enormous as we continue to globalize and connect all points of the world to all other points of the world, both electronically and logistically.

Imagine the opportunity as we connect billions of objects, such as packages, Web-ready television, set-top boxes and telephones in networks where every object touches the others. The enormity of this proposition is almost beyond human belief. It actually holds out the one great promise for solving some of the seemingly insurmountable problems that our children and grandchildren will face — problems ranging from global warming to poverty and world hunger to the need for economies to continue to grow if we're going to continue to raise the standard of living throughout the world. With both physical distribution and telecommunications networks working together, I believe we can provide solutions such as better education and training, better understanding of others' needs and wants through improved communication, and new money and payment systems that will allow the economies of the world to work together more smoothly.

Networks will enable nonindustrialized parts of the world to receive, at affordable prices, the same kinds of goods and services as the industrialized parts of the world. As we build these big networks, the incremental costs become less. Businesses can pinpoint markets through these marvelous new point-to-point networks and provision people with communications devices. As more people find it affordable to be part of the network, a whole new networked economy will be created. The great opportunity before both FedEx and Netscape is the integration of the physical distribution and electronic networks to bring even more of the power of service organizations to the people of the world. The phenomenal success of Federal Express to date is a true testament to the power of these integrated networks.

Congratulations to Federal Express on its 25th year as a leader in the networked economy. I wish you all the best for the next 25.

JIM BARKSDALE IS PRESIDENT AND CEO OF NETSCAPE COMMUNICATIONS CORPORATION.

"From now on the world will be split between the fast and the slow."

Alvin Toffler

LOOKING BACK ON 25 YEARS at the forefront of a dynamic and evolving industry, two things have remained constant at FedEx: change, and the ability and willingness of our employees to embrace change on behalf of our customers.

From our ambitious early days in 1973, FedEx people have worked tirelessly and dreamed boundlessly to stretch our service capabilities and the scope of our network. Today, FedEx ranks among the networks that keep the global marketplace moving, thriving and connected.

Looking forward to a new century of challenges and opportunities, FedEx recognizes that the pace of change will continue, if not intensify. We know that our customers — corporations and small businesses that are defining the Information Age economy — will continue to seek and reward those carriers that consistently find new, technology-smart methods of moving materials and managing information in ways that add value, negate distance and optimize time.

This 25th-anniversary book is a reflection on the past achievements of FedEx employees, and also a celebration of our shared vision for the future. A future in which we at FedEx will further expand our network, sharpen our technology tools and broaden and deepen our portfolio of services, so customers worldwide can satisfy virtually all their distribution and logistics requirements with a single source. The world leader. FedEx.

We can visualize this future with confidence based on the proven dedication and creativity of our employees. Because at the end of the day, when a customer taps into the FedEx network to send an important express shipment to a far-off destination, that customer is tapping into our greatest strength: our people. People who've delivered packages, freight — and remarkable results — for a quarter century.

FREDERICK W. SMITH
CHAIRMAN, PRESIDENT AND
CHIEF EXECUTIVE OFFICER OF FDX CORPORATION
FOUNDER OF FEDERAL EXPRESS CORPORATION

How Time Flies: FedEx Delivers the 21st Century.
Copyright © Federal Express Corporation, 1998.
All rights reserved. No portion of this book may
be reprinted or reproduced without permission
from FedEx. Editor: Marla J. Kinney. Writers:
Jeannie Ralston, Jack El-Hai, Vince Giorgi.
Designers: Sandy Rumreich, Cindy Richter.
Major photography: David Burnett, Steve
Cook, Robb Kendrick, Steve McCurry, Roger Tully,
Nancy Welsch and FedEx Archives. Produced by
Hanley-Wood Custom Publishing.

The editors would like to acknowledge the
following FedEx employees for their contributions
to this book: Myron Lowery, Bill Margaritis, Sandra
Muñoz and Greg Rossiter. In addition, FedEx
Corporate Communications wishes to thank all the
other FedEx employees and honored essayists
who contributed to this book.

CREDITS: *Fast Cycle Time: How to Align Purpose,
Strategy and Structure for Speed* by Christopher
Meyer, reprinted with the permission of The Free
Press, a Division of Simon & Schuster, copyright
© 1993 by Christopher Meyer; *Competing Against
Time: How Time-Based Competition Is Reshaping
Global Markets* by George Stalk Jr. and Thomas
M. Hout, reprinted with the permission of The Free
Press, a Division of Simon & Schuster, copyright
© 1990 by The Free Press; *2020 VISION: Transform
Your Business Today to Succeed in Today's
Economy* by Stan Davis and Bill Davidson, reprint-
ed with the permission of Simon & Schuster,
copyright © 1991 by William H. Davidson and
Stanley M. Davis; *Reengineering the Corporation*
by Michael Hammer and James Champy, copyright
© 1993 by Michael Hammer & James Champy,
reprinted by permission of HarperCollins Publishers,
Inc.; *The World On Time* by James Wetherbe,
Knowledge Exchange, Santa Monica, Calif. (1996);
Forbes® Great Minds of Business. © Forbes Inc.
1997. *Powershift* by Alvin Toffler, reprinted by permission of Bantam Books, a division of Bantam
Doubleday Dell. Quote on pp. 112-116 reprinted by
permission of *Harvard Business Review.* Excerpt
from George Stalk Jr., "Time—The Next Source of
Competitive Advantage" in (July-August 1988),
page 41. Copyright © 1988 by the President and
Fellows of Harvard College; all rights reserved.

ALBANIA ALGERIA AMERICAN SAMOA ANDORRA ANGOLA ANGUILLA ANTIGUA A

BANGLADESH BARBADOS BARBUDA BELARUS BELGIUM BELIZE BENIN BERMUDA

BURKINA FASO BURMA BURUNDI CAMBODIA CAMEROON CANADA CAPE VERDE C

COLOMBIA CONGO COOK ISLANDS COSTA RICA CROATIA CURACAO CYPRUS CZECH R

REPUBLIC ECUADOR EGYPT EL SALVADOR ENGLAND EQUATORIAL GUINEA ERITREA

POLYNESIA GABON GAMBIA GEORGIA GERMANY GHANA GIBRALTAR GREECE GREE

HAITI HONDURAS HONG KONG HUNGARY ICELAND INDIA INDONESIA NORTHERN

KAZAKHSTAN KENYA SOUTH KOREA KUWAIT KYRGYZSTAN LAOS LATVIA LEBANON

MALAWI MALAYSIA MALDIVES REPUBLIC MALI MALTA MARSHALL ISLANDS MARTIN

MONTSERRAT MOROCCO MOZAMBIQUE MYANMAR NAMIBIA NEPAL NETHERLANDS

NORWAY OMAN PAKISTAN PALAU PANAMA PAPUA NEW GUINEA PARAGUAY PERU

RUSSIA RWANDA SABA ST. BARTHELEMY ST. CROIX ST. EUSTATIUS ST. JOHN ST. L

SAUDI ARABIA SCOTLAND SENEGAL SEYCHELLES SIERRA LEONE SINGAPORE SLO

SWAZILAND SWEDEN SWITZERLAND SYRIA TAIWAN TANZANIA THAILAND TOGO TRI

UKRAINE UNITED ARAB EMIRATES UNITED STATES URUGUAY UZBEKISTAN VANUATU V